Contents

1 Muhammad ﷺ 2

2 The Qur'an and its teachings 16

3 Islamic worship 30

4 Social Islam 66

Notes

As a mark of respect, Muslims may add 'Peace be upon him' when they refer to the Prophet Muhammad and other prophets. In this book it is abbreviated as ﷺ.

Dates from the Muslim calendar are shown as AH (*Anno Hegira*); others are shown as CE (Common Era), which is equivalent to AD in the Christian calendar.

Quotations from the Qur'an have been printed in italics, whereas teachings of the Prophet ﷺ himself are in normal script.

Muhammad ﷺ

The Arab Muhammad ﷺ (c. 570–632 CE) was the founder of the world religion known as Islam and is honoured as the last prophet in a long series of messengers of Allah, the Muslim name for God. Over a period of about 22 years Muhammad ﷺ received messages from God, often through the angel Jibril (Gabriel), and these collected revelations form the Qur'an, the holy book of Islam. The teachings of the Qur'an restored the faith of the earlier monotheistic prophets such as Ibrahim (Abraham) ﷺ and Jesus ﷺ.

Muhammad ﷺ was a political and military leader as well as a religious one. The Prophet ﷺ set up what was essentially the first Islamic state in Madinah (Medina), but often had to combat a great deal of resistance both to the new religion and his growing political power. After his death, as Islam rapidly spread throughout the Arabian peninsula and beyond, a fierce dispute arose between the direct descendants of Muhammad ﷺ and other Muslim leaders, eventually leading to the major split between Sunni and Shi'a Islam.

His birth and early life

The Prophet Muhammad ﷺ was a direct descendant of the Biblical patriarch Ibrahim/Abraham ﷺ, through his eldest son Isma'il ﷺ. He was born in Makkah (Mecca), in what is now Saudi Arabia, in around 570 CE, a member of the Hashim clan of the Quraysh tribe. His father, Abdullah, a merchant, died before he was born, and his mother, Amina, died when he was only six years old, leaving him an orphan. He was reared first by his grandfather, Abd al-Muttalib, a man famous for his saintly life, and then by his merchant uncle, Abu Talib. The only person with him from his first breath to his last was his Abyssinian nurse Barakah (Umm Ayman), who he always called 'Mother'.

At this time, the people of Arabia were mainly superstitious pagans, plus Jewish and Christian populations, especially on the border with Syria and Yemen. Many Arabs lived nomadic lives on traditionally claimed territories, and there were only a few key cities such as Makkah, Yathrib and Taif. Makkah was a wealthy trading post that grew up around the Ka'bah shrine, originally to the One God but then taken over by idol worshippers.

Muhammad ﷺ grew up a particularly devout and honourable man, a believer in One God, like his grandfather. He worked first as a shepherd, and then as a merchant, becoming well known and respected, and earning the nickname 'al-Amin' ('the Trustworthy One') for his piety, honesty, fair dealing, and practical common sense. He was a founding member of an Order of Chivalry (the Hilf al-Fudul) dedicated to bringing justice and protecting the rights of the poor and weak.

Aged 25, he was employed by a wealthy tradeswoman, Khadijah, who, after a short while, offered herself in marriage to him, although she was in her forties. She had been married twice before and had at least five children living. Despite the age difference, they were very happily married and had at least six children of their own. Their two sons (Qasim and Abdullah) died as infants, leaving Muhammad ﷺ with four daughters – Zaynab, Ruqaiyyah, Umm Kulthum and Fatimah. Only Fatimah survived him, and only by a few months.

He fostered two boys, his cousin Ali from the age of four, and Khadijah's slave Zayd ibn Harithah from the age of 14. In due course Ali married Fatimah. Even though polygamy was normal among Arabs at this time, Muhammad ﷺ never considered any other marriage while Khadijah lived.

His call to be a Prophet ﷺ

His new wealth and security gave him much more time to devote to prayer and meditation. It had been his grandfather's practice to withdraw to the solitude of the mountains around Makkah, often for several days, and to remain in this seclusion during the entire month of Ramadan; now Muhammad ﷺ was able to do the same. He particularly favoured the Cave of Hira on Jabal Nur (the 'Mount of Light') a two-hour climb for those fetching his provisions. During the Ramadan month of the year 610 CE, when he was around 40 years old, something happened that changed his life completely.

A presence he identified as the angel Jibril (Gabriel) was suddenly there with him, and he was shown words and ordered to recite them. He protested that he was not a learned man and could not read them, but the angel insisted, and suddenly Muhammad ﷺ was given to understand what the words said. He was ordered to learn them, and repeat them to others. Thus came the first revelation of the verses now collected in book form, known as the Qur'an (the Recitation).

The night this happened was towards the end of Ramadan, which later became the Islamic month of fasting. The night is known as *Laylat ul-Qadr*. It is usually celebrated on the 27th night of Ramadan, although the exact date is not known.

From this moment Muhammad's ﷺ life was entirely in the hands of Him who had called him to be a prophet, and to spend the rest of his days in His service. Modestly, he commenced his mission by repeating the messages to a small circle of his family and friends, but reports of what had happened spread like wildfire.

The first convert was a woman, his wife Khadijah; the first male convert was Ali (then aged ten), and the first adult males were his best friend, the merchant Abu Bakr, and his foster son Zayd.

The way of life he taught became known as 'Islam', which means 'submission to the will of God', and his followers were known as Muslims, 'those who submit'. Allah, the Muslim name for God, simply means 'the Almighty'.

After the first few visions, and the initial whirlwind of excitement, everything stopped. To his dismay and embarrassment, the Prophet ﷺ spent the next two years with no further angelic visitation or message, a period of trial and testing when he was not sure of the implications of what had happened to him. Then, at last, the messages began again, and continued for the rest of his life, a prophetic ministry of some 22 years.

His early mission

At first, the Prophet ﷺ did not preach in public, but spoke privately to those who were interested, or who had noticed the change in him. The particular way of Muslim prayer was revealed to him, and he began to practise this daily, which again drew comment from those who saw him. When he was given the instruction to begin preaching in public, he was ridiculed and abused as people scoffed at what he was saying and doing.

Also, many of the Quraysh tribesmen – who had a vested interest in the Ka'bah shrine, since they provided the many pagan pilgrims with food, water, lodging and protection en route – were seriously alarmed, as they realized his insistence on the One True God would undermine the prestige and credibility of the shrine, if people were converted to the Prophet's ﷺ ways and began to abandon the worship of idols.

Some of the Prophet's ﷺ own uncles became his chief opponents, vilifying and ridiculing him, and stirring up trouble for those who had been converted. There were many instances of torture and abuse, particularly against slaves and women who joined the 'new' religion. The first martyr of Islam was a slave woman, Sumayyah, and the first *mu'adhin* (caller to prayer) was a negro slave, Bilal, who was rescued by Abu Bakr from being left to die in the blazing sun with a huge rock on his chest.

The year of sorrow

In the year 619, the Prophet's ﷺ beloved wife, Khadijah, died. She had been his most ardent supporter and helper. In the same year his uncle Abu Talib, an eminent sheikh able to protect him from the worst persecution of the tribes, also died. The grief-stricken Prophet ﷺ left Makkah and tried to make a fresh start in the town of Taif, but was also rejected there.

Now aged 50, he married a devout widow, Sawdah, one of the first Muslim converts, and Aishah, the little daughter of his friend Abu Bakr, who the Prophet ﷺ had known and loved since the day she was born. She was far too young for physical marriage at this time, but was engaged in a non-physical relationship that was quite traditional.

The 'Night of Ascent'

In the same year the Prophet ﷺ experienced the second most important night of his life, the *Laylat ul-Miraj* or 'Night of Ascent'.

This experience bore no resemblance to the Christian belief in the Ascension to Heaven of the body of Jesus ﷺ after his death and resurrection. The Prophet's ﷺ experience occurred during his lifetime. It is not clear whether it was a vision, dream or psychic happening, but in it he was woken from where he lay sleeping and taken by a *buraq*, a miraculous beast, to Jerusalem. From the ruins of the old Jewish Temple on Mount Zion, a way was opened for him through the heavens until he approached the Throne of God, in a region even he and the angel Jibril, who was accompanying him, were not allowed to enter.

It was during this night that the rules for the compulsory prayer five times per day (the *salat*) were revealed to him.

They became the central part of the faith and have formed the keystone of Muslim life ever since.

The experience brought great comfort and strength to the Prophet ﷺ and confirmed that Allah had not deserted him, or left him to suffer alone. After this night, he lived for another 12 years, with no similar experience.

The Hijrah – Migration to Madinah

The Prophet's ﷺ fortunes now changed dramatically. Although still persecuted and ridiculed in Makkah, his message had spread rapidly. Some of the elders of the oasis of Yathrib invited him to leave Makkah to be their honoured leader and judge. This region was the home of both Arab and Jewish people and there had been constant conflict between them. They hoped Muhammad ﷺ would bring them peace.

The Prophet ﷺ immediately advised his Muslim followers to go ahead, while he remained in Makkah as long as possible to allay suspicions. Their empty houses were soon noted, however, as they slipped away. He was almost the last Muslim to leave. Without the restraining hand of Abu Talib, he knew the Quraysh would feel free to attack him, even to kill him, and this is what he realized they intended to do. They had no intention of letting him leave the city, or be received with honour anywhere else.

The Prophet's ﷺ move was not without some drama. Ali bravely volunteered to stay in his bed as a decoy, and the Prophet ﷺ left with Abu Bakr. A price was put on their heads. On a couple of occasions the Quraysh nearly succeeded in capturing him, but eventually they arrived at the outskirts of Yathrib. This emigration was known as the *hijrah*.

So many people rushed out to offer him refuge in their homes that he was embarrassed by their kindness, and left the choice of place to his famous camel *al-Qaswah*, which hesitated a few times, then finally stopped by a place where dates were spread out to dry. This was instantly offered to the Prophet ﷺ, and became the site of his mosque and his home. The town took a new name – *Madinat al-Nabi*, the 'town of the Prophet' – which is now shortened to Madinah (Medina).

The Muslims who had preceded him from Makkah and made their own *hijrah* were known as *Muhajirun*, the 'emigrants'. They were in the position of refugees, having left all their belongings behind. The Prophet ﷺ appealed to the people of Madinah to take them in and offer them homes. Those who volunteered to help the Makkan Muslims were known as *Ansars*, the 'helpers'.

The Prophet ﷺ as ruler

The Prophet ﷺ then set about creating a charter which would enable all the disputing tribes and factions in Madinah to accept him as head of state and abide by his decisions. He ruled that all the citizens should be free to practise their own religion in peaceful co-existence, without fear of persecution or ill-favour. He asked only that if there was any aggression or tyranny, they should join together and cooperate in the face of the enemy.

The previous tribal laws of both Arabs and Jews were replaced by the basic principle of general justice for all, irrespective of class, colour or creed. At first, the Jewish tribespeople of Madinah accepted the Prophet's ﷺ rule; no Jew was ever forced to become a Muslim, and they were treated as equal citizens of Madinah and their own faith was protected. Later, trouble broke out when two Jewish tribes did not keep the principle of supporting Madinah against attacks from outside, and those individuals were condemned as traitors.

The Prophet's ﷺ way of life

Every act and detail of the Prophet's ﷺ life was of the greatest interest to those around him; his recorded deeds and sayings, the *hadiths*, ran into many thousands.

Although he was now ruler of a city-state, and in receipt of increasing wealth and influence, the Prophet ﷺ never lived like a king. His home consisted of simple mud-brick houses that were built for his wives; he never actually had even a room of his own.

Adjacent to these little houses was a courtyard with a well that became the mosque, the meeting place for the Muslim faithful.

He was never arrogant or superior, despite his position as leader; he never made people feel small, unwanted or embarrassed. He urged his followers to live kindly and humbly, releasing slaves as far as they were able, and generally showing practical charity, without thinking of reward. He said: 'Feed, for the love of Allah, the destitute, the orphan and the prisoner, saying: We feed you for the sake of Allah alone, desiring no reward from you, or thanks.' Much of his time was spent visiting the sick, comforting the bereaved, and counselling people with problems.

All his recorded words and actions reveal him as a man of gentleness, kindness, good humour and excellent common sense, with a great love for all people, especially children, and for animals. He had an implacable sense of justice, but ruled with humility and compassion. He was not only treated by his followers with enormous respect – he was deeply loved.

The Prophet's ﷺ life of prayer

The Prophet's ﷺ life was spent virtually in a constant state of prayer, and in teaching his followers. Apart from the five compulsory prayers, which he led in the mosque, the Prophet ﷺ also spent many hours in private prayer and contemplation, sometimes during the greater part of the night, snatching a little sleep towards the end of the night before being woken for the pre-sunrise prayer (the *fajr*).

Like many in a hot climate, the Prophet ﷺ made up for loss of sleep by taking a siesta during the heat of the day, after the midday prayer (the *zuhr*). Late afternoon was the time when the heat dropped again, and a major time of prayer – with the *asr* as the light began to change, and the *maghrib* after sunset. The last formal prayer was the *isha* during the hours of darkness.

The Prophet's ﷺ family

In the last ten years of his life, the Prophet ﷺ took at least 10 other women and their children into his household, all but two of whom had suffered the loss of their original spouses through death or divorce.

Unlike Khadijah, the later wives of the Prophet shared his life as ruler of Madinah. However, they had no luxuries but were expected to follow his devout and simple way of life, and to make enormous personal sacrifice. They became known as the 'Mothers of the Faithful', and lived in a row of tiny houses along the wall of the Prophet's ﷺ mosque, at the centre of the Muslim religious community.

By his later wives, the Prophet ﷺ had one further child of his own, a son Ibrahim, who, like his two sons by Khadijah, died in infancy.

His four daughters all married and three of them bore children. Of them, the most famous was his youngest daughter, Fatimah, who married Ali and gave him two grandsons, Hasan and Husayn, and two granddaughters, Zaynab and Umm Kulthum.

Jihad

The Prophet ﷺ was a man of peace and reconciliation, and would have preferred it if he had been left in peace in Madinah, but sadly, the opposition from the Quraysh tribes continued and he was obliged to take part in sporadic warfare. Even so, the total amount of time he spent fighting only came to a few months.

His two most important early battles – Badr and Uhud – only took a single day. The Muslims won the first, but the second was a stalemate. As a result of this warfare, the many rules of conduct of war and treatment of prisoners were laid down for Muslims, the rules of *jihad*.

Jihad was never to be military activity for the sake of nationalism, tyranny or aggrandizement, but primarily for defensive reasons, and only until the enemy could be brought to peace. During the Prophet's battles, many of the enemy were converted to his side, impressed by the Muslim chivalry, courage and faith in God.

In March 627, Abu Sufyan, the chief sheikh of Makkah, raised a massive force of 10,000 men and advanced on Madinah, buoyed up by support from a Jewish tribe in the Madinah outskirts that had agreed to the charter, but then turned traitor and decided to oust the Prophet ﷺ. This was called the Battle of the Trench, since the Prophet had a huge ditch speedily constructed to protect the city. After a two-week siege, the opposition withdrew, giving the Prophet ﷺ a moral victory, for the eyes of Arabia had been upon him, and he had shown that even this vast army could not defeat him.

Pilgrimage to Makkah

In March 628 the Prophet ﷺ journeyed to Makkah with some 1,400 followers, all unarmed, in pilgrim dress of two simple white cloths. Although an increasing number of the citizens of Makkah had by now accepted Islam, the Prophet's ﷺ followers were still refused entry. Instead of making trouble, they offered their sacrifices outside Makkah, at a place called Hudaybiyah. The Quraysh chief, Suhayl, who had replaced Abu Sufyan, came out and negotiated a treaty to keep the peace for ten years.

The Muslims repeated the pilgrimage in 629, and this time were allowed to visit the ancient tribal holy places undisturbed while the Makkans vacated the city and watched them from the hills. The impressive Muslim behaviour made many new converts.

The surrender of Makkah

The Prophet ﷺ then began to plan for the spread of Islam. He dictated letters to the leaders of the surrounding kingdoms, inviting them to consider Islam – the Roman Byzantine Emperor, the Persian Emperor, the rulers of Egypt, Abyssinia and many leading chiefs – but of these only the Abyssinian Negus accepted and was converted. The letter to the Muqawqis of Egypt still exists and may be seen in the Topkapi Museum, Istanbul.

In November 629 the Makkans attacked one of the tribes that was allied with the Muslims, giving the Prophet ﷺ, grounds to march against them. In 630 his army camped outside Makkah and Abu Sufyan (whose widowed daughter Umm Habibah had become one of the Prophet's ﷺ wives) came over to his side. The Prophet ﷺ

promised a general amnesty if the Makkans would formally submit, declaring that all who took refuge with Abu Sufyan or who shut their doors on the battle would be safe. In the event, there was only one skirmish in which 11 people lost their lives before the surrender.

The Prophet ﷺ entered the city in triumph, went straight to the Ka'bah, and performed the ritual circumambulation seven times. He then entered the shrine and destroyed all the idols.

All the hereditary territories were left in the hands of their accustomed guardians, and the Prophet ﷺ asked followers whose abandoned property in Makkah had been seized when they moved to Madinah not to claim it back. Uthman ibn Talhah, who had once refused Muhammad ﷺ entry to the Ka'bah and persecuted him, was given back the key to the shrine, and it remains with his family to this day. One by one the Quraysh swore their fealty to the Prophet ﷺ, and were pardoned. Only ten people, who were also guilty of murder or incitement to murder, were condemned to death, but of these only four were executed.

The final pilgrimage and the last Sermon

The Prophet ﷺ did not live long to enjoy a peaceful rule. His army was obliged to conduct further warfare against tribes that attacked them – tribes that had been shocked by the desecration of their idols at Makkah – before he was able to return to his home in Madinah.

Events outside Arabia worked to the advantage of Islam. The western part of the Roman Empire was overrun by barbarians, and in the east the Byzantines at Constantinople had fallen into confusion through internal conflicts and inefficient rule. The Persian Sassanid Empire (which covered today's Iraq, Iran and Afghanistan) had engaged the Byzantines in conflict for some 30 years, and had successfully captured Jerusalem, but by 630 the Byzantines had retaken it and Persian influence was low, leaving a political vacuum for the warriors of Islam to occupy.

In March 632 the Prophet ﷺ made his one complete Muslim *Hajj* to the Ka'bah shrine, known as the *Hajjat ul-Wida*, the Final Pilgrimage. During this pilgrimage the revelations about the rules of the Hajj were given to him, which are followed by all Muslims to this day. Up to this time pagans had been allowed to visit the Ka'bah as well as Muslims, but now all pagan influence was removed, and only Muslims were allowed into the city.

When the Prophet ﷺ arrived at Mount Arafat for the 'Stand before Allah', he delivered what is known as his 'Final Sermon'. The summarized text of this famous teaching can be found in mosques all over the world:

O people, listen carefully to what I say, for I do not know whether, after this year, I shall ever be amongst you again. Listen carefully, and report my words to those who cannot be here today.

Regard the life and property of every Muslim as a sacred trust ... Hurt no one, so that no one may hurt you. Remember that you will indeed meet your Lord, and that He will reckon your deeds ... You will neither inflict nor suffer injustice ... O men, remember that you have rights with regard to your women, but they also have rights over you. Remember that you have taken them as your wives only under Allah's trust and with His permission ... Treat them well and be kind to them, for they are your partners and committed helpers ...

O believers, worship Allah, say your five daily prayers; fast during the month of Ramadan, and give your wealth in zakah. Perform Hajj, if you can afford to ...

An Arab has no superiority over a non-Arab; a white has no superiority over a black, nor a black over a white, except in piety and good deeds. Every Muslim is a brother (or sister) to every other Muslim ...

No prophet or apostle will come after me, and no new faith will be born ... I leave behind me two things, the Qur'an and the Sunnah; if you follow these, you will never go astray.[1]

[1] Shi'ite sources say the two things were the Qur'an and his family.

At the end, he received his final revelation:

Today I have perfected your religion for you, and I have
completed My blessing upon you; and I have approved
Islam as your religion.

(Surah 5:5)

There was a silence, and then the voice of Bilal rose over the enormous hushed crowd, calling them to prayer.

The death of the Prophet ﷺ

Back in Madinah, the Prophet ﷺ was informed that a huge Byzantine army was massing on the Syrian border, but he became ill and developed a heavy fever. He continued to lead the prayers in the mosque as long as he was able, supported by Ali, and when too ill he requested Abu Bakr to take his place. The army was entrusted to Usamah, the 17-year-old son of Zayd by the Prophet's ﷺ nurse Umm Ayman.

He did not recover, and eventually collapsed. His wives realized that he wished to be with Aishah, and moved him to her room, where he died in her arms[2] on 8 June 632 (12 Rabi'ul Awwal, 11 AH, in the Muslim calendar).

He was not an old man – only 63 years old. (Many of his friends lived into their eighties.) His last words were said to have been: 'I have chosen the most exalted Companions, in Paradise.' He was buried in Aishah's room, which is now a shrine and part of the modern mosque complex at Madinah. May peace be upon him.

[2] Shi'ite sources state he died in Ali's arms. Both were present at this sad time.

2

the Qur'an and its teachings

Muslims hold the Qur'an in deepest reverence, since they believe it to contain the revelations of God to His final prophet, Muhammad ﷺ, in His direct words. Muhammad ﷺ received the series of revelations over a period of some 22 years, from 610 CE until his death. He recited the revelations to his followers, who memorized them, kept collections of them, and arranged them in the order revealed to them – the word Qur'an itself is thought by Islamic scholars to derive from the Arabic for 'he recited'. The revelations were gathered, checked and sanctioned in book form shortly after the Prophet's ﷺ death.

Muhammad's ﷺ own words and deeds were also gathered into long collections known as hadith. Some of Muhammad's ﷺ sayings are also considered to be revealed by Allah (though not part of the Qur'an). The hadith provide Muslims with a rich treasury of guidance on how to interpret the Qur'an and on numerous ethical, political, and legal issues. Sunni and Shi'a branches of Islam recognize different collections of hadith.

The Qur'an

Writing down the revelations

The *Qur'an* was revealed to the Prophet ﷺ bit by bit over a period of 23 years. Muslims believe that it is the Word of Allah, exactly as the Prophet ﷺ received it, and in this sense it is different from any other of the world's holy books, since they were all created by human authors many years after the deaths of the prophets involved, and were then edited and revised and added to by disciples. The Qur'an contains nothing but the direct revelations from Allah, through the angel Jibril, not one word of it being the creation of the Prophet ﷺ. He was nothing more than the transmitter. (The Prophet's ﷺ own teachings and sayings run into many thousands and are known as *hadiths*.)

As each revelation was given, the verses were learnt by heart and jotted down on whatever materials came to hand: dried-out palm leaves, pieces of broken pottery, ribs and shoulder bones of sheep, bits of animal skin and flat stones.

A single verse is known as an *ayah* (meaning a 'sign'), and a chapter is a *surah* (a step up). There are 114 surahs of varying lengths (all except the ninth beginning with the words '*In the Name of Allah, the Most Compassionate, the Most Merciful*'), and 6,616 ayahs – a total of 78,000 words in Arabic.

The surahs are not in chronological order, however. It is generally accepted that the first words are in surah 96:1–5 and the final words are in surah 5. The order was also something revealed to the Prophet ﷺ, who had to recite the whole collection revealed so far to the angel every Ramadan, and the entire text was checked with the angel twice, shortly before the Prophet ﷺ died.

The first surah is called *al-Fatihah* (the Opening). Each surah is named after some striking incident or word in it, so some have strange names like *al-Baqarah* (the Cow) and *al-Ankabut* (the Spider). Others have names of Allah, for example, *al-Nur* (the Light), *al-Rahman* (the Merciful). The Cow is actually about religious duties, divorce laws and rules governing fair conduct of war.

Compiled as a book

Islam began at a time when books were the property of only the rich, and people had the habit of learning a great deal by heart. Anyone who knew the full text of the Qur'an was known as a *hafiz* (pl. *huffaz*).

After the Prophet's ﷺ death, Abu Bakr requested that the revelations be gathered together, the first complete written version in one book. The Prophet's ﷺ scribe was reluctant to do something the Prophet ﷺ had not authorized, but was eventually persuaded.

He did not alter the messages in any way; no explanations or editorial comments were added. The pages of this text were kept by Abu Bakr, passed to Umar, and then to his daughter, Hafsah the Prophet's ﷺ widow, and were known as the *mushaf* of Hafsah.

When many of the original huffaz had passed away, and Muslims were beginning to write down verses in their dialects, this brought with it the danger of personal interpretation, misinterpretation and alternative versions (*qira'ah*). Uthman realized the Revelation might become corrupted, since all translations and editions were dependent upon the skills of the translator or editor; so in 651 he ordered that all texts which individuals owned were either checked for full agreement against Hafsah's text, or destroyed.

Uthman had six copies of this 'standard' text inscribed on the specially prepared skins of sacrificed goats. He kept one for himself in Madinah, and sent the others to the chief Muslim centres – Makkah, Kufa, Damascus, Cairo, and Sana. Since then all texts have been identical, and handed down unaltered; and there is probably no other book in the world which has remained 12 centuries with so pure a text.

If non-Arabic-speaking Muslims wish to read the Qur'an translated into their own languages, it is best done with the original Arabic alongside. Muslim scholars all try to master Arabic, and those with no Arabic usually refer to several translations.

How respect is shown to the Qur'an

The Qur'an is not just a book, but the Sacred Text. If Muslims have the space, their Qur'an may be kept in a special room which is kept clean and used only for prayer and reading the holy Text.

When a Qur'an is in the room, Muslims are expected to behave with reverence, so it would not be proper to act indecently, rudely, cruelly or selfishly. The Qur'an imparts an atmosphere of prayer – it is the silent reminder of the Muslim submission to Allah. If a TV or video is in that room any crude, violent or abusive programme content would not be suitable.

While the Qur'an is being recited aloud, Muslims should not speak, eat or drink, smoke, or make any distracting noise. Before touching the Qur'an, Muslims should be in a state of *wudu*, or at least wash their hands. Muslim women would usually cover their heads as for prayer, and a woman who is menstruating or has recently given birth should not touch it.

Before beginning to read, Muslims 'prepare the heart' by consciously thinking about Allah and seeking refuge from Satan (Surah 16:98). They adopt a special position, so that the body is disciplined and alert, often sitting on the floor with the Qur'an on a special stand (called a *rehl* or *kursi*) in front of them. It is disrespectful to place the Qur'an on the floor.

Reading with heart, soul, mind and strength is known as *tilawah*, and the practice of correct pronunciation (usually learned in the mosque school or *madrassah*) is called *tajwid* (from *jawad* – to make well, make better or improve). Many Muslims do not speak Arabic, and some initially learn how to recite the verses without understanding what they mean. However, as they progress in Islam they should also learn the meanings, and see how the messages apply to them and how they should alter their own lives. Muslims try to recite or read the entire Qur'an each Ramadan.

When the reading is finished, the Qur'an is put away carefully. It should not be left casually on a table, where someone might put something down on top of it! Muslims are sometimes shocked and offended to see Qur'ans kept and handled in shops, libraries and classrooms.

Translations of the Qur'an into other languages are not regarded as being quite the same thing as the Qur'an itself, and most Muslims in countries where printed books are commonplace are used to the idea of translations being treated casually. It is perhaps important to realize, however, that a Muslim might be horrified rather than flattered by a non-Muslim, not in *wudu*, pulling a Qur'an out of his pocket to have a quick read in the pub!

The sunnah – the Prophet's ﷺ way

The life and example of the Prophet ﷺ is known as the *Sunnah*. The *Shari'ah* is the general title for Islamic law. The *din* (pr. *deen*) is the complete Islamic way of life. The sunnah is known from a study of the *hadiths*, the sayings and teachings of Muhammad ﷺ himself and narratives about him recorded by his friends and handed down to later generations. (In this book, all quotations from the Qur'an are given in italics, and Muhammad's ﷺ teachings in normal script.)

Although the hadiths are not part of the Qur'an revelation, nevertheless they are regarded as vitally important for the full understanding of Islam. They often explain matters or give extra information about the matters ordained by Allah. Once, his wife Aishah was asked about the Prophet's ﷺ customs and way of life. She replied: 'His way of life IS the Qur'an.'

The Qur'an is roughly the same length as the New Testament. The teachings of Muhammad ﷺ himself, if all put together, would work out about the size of the *Encyclopedia Britannica*.

The hadith collections

The two most important collections of hadiths are those of Imam Muhammad b. Isma'il al-Bukhari (died 870 CE), which is regarded as the most authentic (a collection of 7,563 hadiths, covering a vast range of subjects), and Muslim b. al-Hajjaj (died 875 CE) containing 7,422 hadiths. It is easier to read than Bukhari's collection because it arranges all the sayings relevant to one issue together.

Is keeping the sunnah compulsory?

The vast majority of Muslims would never go against the teachings of the Prophet ﷺ as recorded in the hadiths; but occasionally reformers wishing to return to the fundamentals, or people wishing to 'update' Islam take the point of view that it is enough to study the Qur'an, and that if Allah had wished a thing to be known or done, He would have certainly included it in the Qur'an and not left it to chance.

The Prophet ﷺ himself was well aware that this would happen, and gave clear warning against it:

> I have indeed been given the Qur'an and something similar to it besides it. Yet, the time will come when a man leaning on his couch will say: 'Follow the Qur'an only; what you find in it as halal, take as halal, and what you find in it as haram, take it as haram.' But truly, what the Messenger of Allah has forbidden is like what Allah has forbidden.
>
> (Abu Dawud and Darimi)

Many Muslims are so devout that they take all the Prophet's ﷺ *sunnat* (recommendations) as *fard* (compulsory obligations of Islam). However, scholars do make a difference between the two on these grounds: if a fard is missed, then the Muslim has committed a sin for which he or she would be accountable, and if the fard is done, they have done good for which they will be rewarded; but on the other hand, if a Muslim does something sunnah, he or she will be rewarded for it, but there is no punishment if it is omitted. This is a very important difference.

The key teachings of Islam

Tawhid and shirk

There are three basic doctrines about God in Islam: One-ness, Transcendence, and Immanence.

God's Unity or One-ness is known as *tawhid*, 'There is no God but One'. Muslims reason that if God is the First Cause, Creator and Supreme Force in the universe, there can only be One by definition – it is impossible to have two 'supremes' or 'first causes'.

Nothing is remotely like God, and nothing can be compared to Him. Nothing shares His power, and He certainly does not have partners, or any kind of 'family'. The name al-Lah is the name also used for God by Arab Christians. It means 'the Almighty', 'the Supreme'.

He is Allah (the Supreme), the One. Allah is Eternal and Absolute. None is born of Him. He is Unborn. There is none like unto Him.

(Surah 112)

God is only referred to as 'He' because it is traditional. 'He' has no gender; this is why Muslims prefer to use the word 'Allah' rather than 'God'.

Many times Allah is called *Rabb*, or Lord; but never once in the entire 23 years of revelations did He call Himself *Abb*, or Father. This cannot have been accidental. The word 'Father' has human and sexual connotations, and although Muslims are aware of God in an intimate and personal way, they think of Him as Creator rather than Father.

Allah, the Supreme knows and sees everything. He is totally 'other' from His created universe, outside time, eternal, without beginning or end.

No vision can grasp Him, but His grasp is over all vision. He is above all comprehension, yet is acquainted with all things.

(Surah 6:103)

He is beyond the limits of the human mind. It is impossible for humans to imagine what He is like, except as He chooses to reveal it. Our senses always present a limited picture of reality; for example, we think we can touch and see solids, but the microscope reveals something completely different. Allah revealed that He is absolute Order, Justice, Mercy, Truth and Love, and many other concepts.

As well as being transcendent, God is also immanent (*aqrab* – nearer), closer to us than our innermost thoughts, more bound up with us than our own bloodstream. He is near to every person equally, since He is everywhere, in the sense that there is no place that is without His presence.

He is the Owner of everything; what humans think they own is allotted to them by God's will, a gift, and should be used in order to do His will, and must be given back to God in due course.

The love and compassion of Allah

God is not only Creator, He is also Judge, and the eternal fate of every living being lies in His 'hands'. Thankfully, the justice of Allah is not the same as that of human beings, who have incomplete knowledge, or who can be vengeful. God knows every thought and motive, every influence acting upon a person. The nature of Allah, repeated over and over again in the revelation, is Love and Compassion. (*Allah, ar-Rahman ar-Rahim*.)

His mercy is far greater than any humans have the right to expect, or that they show to each other.

> *If God punished us according to what we deserve, He would leave on earth not one living thing.*

(Surah 34:45; 16:61)

Many humans, of course, find this hard to accept, either because they are too proud, or too hard-hearted, or too despairing, or for many other reasons. Nevertheless, Allah assures us of His mercy constantly throughout the Qur'an and hadiths.

The unseen

The universe consists of that which is seen and understood by our five senses, and that which is unseen (known as *al-Ghayb*). What we see and understand is only the tip of the iceberg in the vastness of God's creation.

Angels are the agents and servants of God, the means by which He governs the universe and the channels by which humans become aware of Him. They do not have free-will, but carry out God's wishes. They are sometimes seen by people in times of crisis; many sensitive people feel aware of their presence when they pray and meditate. They may take any shape or form.

A few angels are named and have specific roles: Jibril (Gabriel) brings messages to the chosen ones, and is frequently referred to as the 'holy spirit' in the Qur'an; Mika'il (Michael), is the protector of holy places and life-sustainer in times of trouble; Azra'il takes away the souls of the dying; Israfil is the angel who calls the souls on Judgement Day; Munkar and Nakir are the questioners; Malik, the keeper of Hell; Ridwan, the keeper of Paradise.

Jinn are also non-physical beings, and they can be either good or evil, having free-will like humans. They are thought to inhabit unclean places, and can often frighten and confuse human beings by involving themselves in their lives and homes. Occasionally they attempt to possess human bodies and have to be exorcized. They are not always malevolent, however, and Surah 72 mentions jinn that were converted to Islam.

The Devil (*Shaytan* or *Iblis*) is not a fallen angel in Islamic tradition, but the chief of the jinn. He became the origin of evil through pride, disobedience and rebellion when he refused God's command to honour the newly created humans because he thought he knew better than God. Out of jealousy, he became the enemy of all humans, determined to lead people's hearts and minds away from God. Evil is never equal to Good.

Another order of beings mentioned in the Qur'an are the *huris*, or 'pure companions' of Paradise. These are not our loved ones made young again, nor a supply of virgins to gratify the lusts of the deceased, but 'spirit beings' who know us as our soul-forms, who both miss us when we live on earth, and welcome us when we return to our eternal abode. (Surah 56:22)

Human beings

So far as we know, human beings are the highest physical creations of Allah, and possess both material and spiritual characteristics. Each being has a distinct individual soul (the *rouh*). It is the soul, and not the body the soul lives in, that is the real person.

Every human being consists of 'earth' – that is, material stuff that is constantly coming into being, 'dying' and being replenished – in order to be the temporary 'body' of an individual soul. Keeping this body alive requires continual interaction with the environment (through breathing and eating, for example), and when the soul departs, all the constituent parts of each body become separate again, disintegrate and are recycled by the 'earth'.

Adam and Eve, or evolution?

Muslims believe that human beings are all descended from an original soul created by God and then divided into male and female (Surah 4.1). As regards the theory of evolution, it is as yet unproven and remains no more than a theory, for which there is debatable evidence; apes were created in their own image, and still exist as apes, and so on. Many Muslims accept the notion of 'intelligent' or 'guided evolution', but believe that all scientific theories should be studied with an open mind, since today's 'facts' are often quickly out of date with new discoveries.

It is usually accepted that the first created humans were Adam ﷺ and Eve. The Qur'an does indeed state that Adam ﷺ was created without parents, from 'clay', which may symbolize that human beings are made of or dependent upon humus. The tradition about the woman being created from Adam's ﷺ rib is not part of the Qur'an; the Prophet ﷺ referred to it with some humour when counselling male Companions not to try straightening them, as they would snap.

Humans have an allotted time-span of life on earth, over which they have no control. They are created with equal rights and are equally loved by God, but do not have equal talents or characteristics. Because they exercise free-will they can love and be kind, or hate and be destructive. Their worth in Islam is not measured in intelligence or status, but in submission to God and right living.

Risalah – revelation

If the Muslim's duty is to serve God and do His will, it is God's duty to explain clearly what that will is, otherwise the individual cannot be held responsible for their choices (Surah 17:15). *Risalah* is the channel of communication from Allah. A prophet who merely taught and did not leave writings is a *nabi*, and one who left writings is a *rasul*.

Before the Blessed Muhammad ﷺ there was a whole series of prophets, sent to people of all times and races with messages suitable for those who heard them. The 26 named in the Qur'an include 23 Biblical prophets, among them Noah (Nuh), Abraham (Ibrahim), Moses (Musa), John the Baptist (Yahya ibn Zakriyah) and Jesus ('Isa) (may peace be upon all of them). The great leaders of other monotheistic faiths may have been among the thousands of unnamed prophets.

Four Divinely Revealed books are mentioned in the Qur'an: the *Sahifa* or scrolls dictated to Abraham ﷺ, the *Tawrat* (or Torah) revealed to Moses ﷺ, the *Zabur* (or Psalms) of David ﷺ, and the *Injil* (or Gospel) revealed to Jesus ﷺ. The first is completely lost, and Muslims believe that the others are not to be identified with the contents of today's Bible, which are compilations and editions written many years after the prophets lived.

It is considered inappropriate to try to guess who were the best prophets, or to elevate any messenger above the human status. All the prophets were messengers from the One and the same God, a single 'chain' or prophecy, and all are to be respected and believed. Jesus ﷺ was the most famous as a miracle worker; Muhammad ﷺ is regarded as the 'seal' of the prophets, and the last messenger. Although many other great teachers have inspired the world throughout history since then, there have been no further prophets in the chain bringing direct revelation from God.

Akhirah – life after death

Muslims believe that the human soul lives only once on Earth, and after death faces a Day of Judgement, and an eventual fate in either Paradise or Hell (*Jannam* and *Jahannam*).

After death the body is buried, but the soul of the good person may experience expanded horizons without limit, while the bad person is cramped in the grave. On the Day, God will resurrect all people, and may choose to recreate their decomposed bodies, down to the details of their individual fingerprints (Surah 45:24; 75:1–4).

None will escape this, if God wills, no matter how they died or what happened to their bodies.

Heaven and Hell are frequently described in graphic physical terms; Heaven, or Paradise, being like a beautiful garden, where people become young again and enjoy untainted pleasures, and Hell being a terrible, scorching place of torment, sorrow and remorse. Although many Muslims take the descriptions literally, there are also clues in the Qur'an that they should rather be considered symbolically, since Heaven and Hell are not physical dimensions at all, and our future state lies beyond the scope of our limited human knowledge.

> *In Heaven, I prepare for the righteous believers what no eye has ever seen, no ear has ever heard, and what the deepest mind could never imagine.*

(Hadith Qudsi, and Surah 32:17)

Islam teaches that God does not wish to send anyone to Hell, and they will only be obliged to go there if they insist on evil living without repentance, and treating the truth of God as a lie. Some Muslims even interpret Hell as being rather like a hospital, where the cure may be painful and drastic, but in the end the patient is made whole. Most accept that the state will be eternal.

> *Their status in Heaven or Hell may last for eternity – but this is subject to God's will and mercy.*

(Surah 11:106–8)

Al-Qadr – pre-destination

Muslims believe that the entire universe is under God's control and direction, therefore nothing can take place without His ordaining it. There cannot be such a thing as a random or chance event (see Surah 35:2; 57:22). Muslims accept that things happen according to our destinies; one often hears the phrase 'It is written' (Ar. *maktub*).

Everything is known (even the number of hairs on your head or how many breaths you will take in your life), and everything that happens is an expression of His will, and has purpose and meaning.

God alone is the source of benefit or harm, and to turn to anything else for protection or help is futile.

This idea of pre-destination is notoriously difficult to reconcile with the concept of free-will, but Islam should not be considered a fatalistic religion. The whole point of sending messengers from God to give revelations is to allow humans to use their free-will; the whole point of human life is a test, which would be totally pointless if God had pre-destined human choices.

> **Indeed Allah declared He would not alter the condition of humans until they changed what was in themselves.**
>
> (Surah 13:11; 8:53)

Fatalism renders people helpless and weakens their sense of responsibility, a criticism frequently made of Muslims who misunderstand the importance of revelation and free-will.

Muslims accept that every breath we take is a gift from God, and He alone knows how many breaths he has allotted to us. Can a person cheat God's will and die at a time other than the one allotted? Muslims accept there is a difference between dying (which happens when God wills) and killing – which is governed by human free-will and natural law.

3

Islamic worship

Islamic worship permeates every aspect of Muslims' lives – from their personal and social lives as husbands and wives, parents and children, to their political and civic lives as citizens and workers. For the pious Muslim, religion is not something confined to special holy days or to special holy places; it is something that is always with them, whatever they are doing and wherever they are. Muslims conceive of themselves as servants of Allah and are always aware of His presence.

The Five Pillars represent the key duties of Sunni Muslims. The Pillars are: *shahadah* (bearing witness to the faith), *salah* (prayer), *sawm* (fasting), *zakh* (alms-giving) and *Hajj* (pilgrimage). Bearing witness, prayer and alms-giving are an everyday part of Muslims' lives. Fasting is a duty during the holy month of Ramadan, while the pilgrimage to Makkah, Islam's holiest site, is a duty that all able-bodied Muslims should fulfil at least once and represents the spiritual and emotional highpoint of their lives.

Worship – ibadah

Ibadah comes from the word '*abad*', meaning a slave or servant. Ibadah is therefore service of Allah, or slavery to Him. Basically, it is what Muslims mean by 'worship'. However, for Muslims, worship is not something confined to special days or particular prayers, but a conscious awareness of God throughout the day, every day, and a conscious desire to carry out His will in every sphere of activity.

The concepts of worship

Ihsan

Muslim worship really begins with the concept of *ihsan* or realization. It is perfectly possible for a human being to go through all sorts of forms of worship, prayer and other ritual without really being truly aware of the presence of God. Human nature being what it is, this rather barren worship can happen to anybody from time to time. However, ihsan implies that a person really is making a conscious effort to be 'in communication' with God.

The Prophet ﷺ stated that ihsan means you should worship God as though you can see Him, for He sees you even though you do not see Him.

Iman

The word *iman* means 'faith'. Asked to define iman, the Prophet ﷺ replied that it was to believe in God, His angels, His books, His prophets, and the Last Day and the decreeing of both good and evil.

Amal

Amal means 'action'. Muslims see no point in academic beliefs or doctrines unless they are translated into action. The whole point of Islam is to submit to Allah and direct your life into carrying out His will to the utmost of your ability.

The concept of amal can actually be divided into two categories. The first is to obey the commands of Allah, as in the practice of the five disciplines known as the 'Five Pillars', which will be described shortly. The second is to do one's best in every aspect of daily life and routine to follow the *sunnah* or practice of the Prophet ﷺ, or at least the principles behind the sunnah (if one is dealing with some aspect of modern society that was beyond the personal experience of the Prophet ﷺ) so that every single thing one does is for the greater glory of God. That way, the Muslim believes he or she will keep on the right path, and will find peace, satisfaction, justice and happiness.

Din (pr. *Deen*)

Putting faith and way of life together is known as the *din*, the total desire to commit to Islam.

Jihad

Jihad is one of the most misunderstood of all aspects of Islam. Most non-Muslims take it to mean military action for the purpose of forcing other people to become Muslims, but this is totally against the principle of Islam, which defends individual liberties. The fact that various persons claiming to be Muslim have acted incorrectly, some even to the extent of horrifying brutality, does not alter this fact, any more than one could judge Christianity by the atrocities of the Ku Klux Klan in the USA.

Islamic jihad in fact insists that oppression for the sake of religion is wrong. Religion should never become an oppressor. People should never be forced to accept things that they do not believe. The whole essence and reason for jihad is to be prepared to sacrifice one's own self in order to fight against tyranny and oppression, to bring freedom and justice and a just peace.

Jihad is often thought to mean only military activity, and obviously it can have a military context, but this is not the true meaning of the word. The definition of jihad according to Qur'an and sunnah is a struggle or an effort that is exerted in order to attain some end or result, any kind of striving which involves either spiritual or personal effort, material resources, or lastly, military means.

A jihad or struggle in the cause of Allah (*fi sabi'l illah*) involves an unceasing effort to eliminate evil in the form of wrong beliefs, ideas, and values that are projected via thoughts, words and deeds – things like racism, abuse, selfishness, laziness, miserliness, aggression and oppression. It could also be a personal struggle involving some form of hard work or effort to accomplish something of value for Allah's sake – such as studying, teaching others, caring for others in trying circumstances, facing up to bullying, even trying to eliminate some harmful personal habit, such as smoking or obesity.

The true jihad is the battle against what Muslims call *dunya* (literally 'the lusts and degradations of worldliness'). The jihad against selfishness, ignorance and corruption is the 'inner' or 'major' jihad (*jihad al-akhbar*) because all evil arises from the desire of the *nafs* or human soul to put self before Allah. Ignorance, arrogance and lack of compassion lie at the root of all evil, are the causes of all corruption, and the sources of all suffering. The opposite of ignorance is knowledge (*ilm*) that gives rise to wisdom (*hiqmah*). This jihad is therefore an act of devotion with the same significance as the Five Pillars of Islam, so much so that it is often called the Sixth Pillar. 'Striving after (the jihad for) knowledge,' said the Prophet ﷺ, 'is the sacred duty of every man and woman' (Ibn Majah).

Ummah

The Prophet ﷺ was told by Allah as part of His revelation to say:

> *O humanity! I am the messenger of God to you all!*
>
> (Surah 7:158)

> *Believers are one single community (ummah), so make peace and reconciliation between two contenders, and have reverence for Allah, that you may receive mercy.*
>
> (Surah 49:10)

The faith of Islam is a universal faith, intended for all people. The worldwide community of Muslims is known as the *ummah*. It extends across all places and ethnic groupings. When Muslims travel around the world, they find they can mix very easily with other Muslims, even if they do not understand their language.

> Declare your jihad on thirteen enemies you cannot
> see – egoism, arrogance, conceit, selfishness, greed, lust,
> intolerance, anger, lying, cheating, gossiping and slandering.
> If you can master and destroy them, then you will be ready
> to fight the enemy you can see.
>
> (al-Ghazzali – note: the thirteenth 'enemy' is not listed)

Taking all these concepts together, ihsan, iman, amal and jihad make up the Muslim concept of *ibadah*; worship of Allah. This is why Islam is not just a matter of ritual, prayers or fasting or feasts; it is the conscious bringing of every moment of the day, every decision, every detail of one's thoughts and actions, into deliberate line with what one accepts as being the will of Allah.

The five pillars

The faith and practice of Islam is often said to rest upon five pillars: bearing witness, prayer, fasting, charity and pilgrimage (shahadah, salah, sawm, zakah and Hajj).

Shahadah – bearing witness

Shahadah is belief in the heart and bearing witness to the faith. It is a simple statement of creed that falls into two parts: that there is no God but Allah (the Almighty, Supreme, the One), and that Muhammad ﷺ is His genuine messenger. It comes from the word '*ash-shadu*' which means 'I declare' or 'I bear witness'.

In Arabic, the words are:

Ash-shadu an la ilaha illallah wa Muhammadar-rasulullah.

When people make this declaration and truly believe it in their hearts, then they have entered the faith. There is no ceremony like a Christian baptism; what counts is the conscious awareness and firm conviction that one genuinely does hold these two beliefs.

Sometimes a new Muslim will talk things over with an *imam* (teacher), or have a course of study sessions; once the new Muslim takes the decision to become Muslim (or realizes that he or she is Muslim), they should declare the faith publicly, in front of two witnesses. From that moment of public witness, they have started on the path of submission to God. Some new Muslims, particularly white ones, like to have a certificate for occasions when proof might be needed. However, shahadah is not just a matter of reciting words; it is something that has to be believed with all one's heart, because following this declaration Muslims are intended to trust God completely, and hand over their lives to His service.

The shahadah is also used for the call to prayer five times per day. If the mosque has a tower, a man known as the *mu'adhin* (or *muezzin*) climbs up and calls aloud:

Allahu Akbar! (four times)
Ash-hadu an la ilaha illallah (twice)
Ash-hadu ana Muhammadar-rasulullah (twice)
Hayya ala-salah (twice)
Hayya ala-falah (twice)
Allahu Akbar (twice)
La ilaha illallah. (once)

God is the Most Great!
I bear witness that there is no God but Allah.
I bear witness that Muhammad is the Prophet of Allah.
Come to prayer!
Come to success (or salvation)!
God is the Most Great!
There is no God but Allah!

At the end of the first prayer of the day the phrase 'It is better to pray than to sleep!' is added – '*as-salatul khairum min an-naum*'.

This call to prayer is known as the *adhan*, and it gives Muslims time to get ready if they are going to attend at the mosque. Just before the actual start of the prayers, a second call to prayer is uttered before the congregation, known as the *iqamah*. It is the same as the adhan, except that the words '*qad qamatis salah*' – 'The prayer has begun' – are added before the final *Allahu Akbars*.

Other times that the shahadah is pronounced are at the birth of a new baby, first thing on waking and last thing before going to sleep at night and, if possible, they are the last words in the hearing of a dying person.

Salah – prayer

O you who believe! Be steadfast in prayer and regular in charity, and whatever good you send forth for your souls before you, you shall find it with God; for truly God sees all that you do.

(Surah 2:110)

Prayer is the second pillar of Islam. Prayer in general terms means being conscious of God and communicating with Him in some way or another, and Muslims try to maintain an attitude of prayer and be constantly aware of God throughout the day. However, the prayer ritual of *salah* (pl. *salat*) is somewhat different from the casual making of appeals to God of a personal nature. It is perhaps better translated in English as 'worship' rather than 'prayer'.

Salah is a ritual of movements and words (each full sequence of which is called a *rakah*), some of the words repeated as part of the regular routine, and others chosen from the Qur'an by the Muslim as he or she wishes.

The five daily prayers are now known as *fajr* (the morning prayer between dawn and sunrise), *zuhr* (just after the height of the midday Sun), *asr* (during the afternoon when the shadows have lengthened), *maghrib* (just after sunset), and *isha* (during the hours of darkness).

The prayer times deliberately avoid the exact times delineated by sunrise, midday and sunset because of their pagan connotations of Sun worship. At those exact times, Muslims are actually ordered not to pray. However, the salat are obviously related to the Sun's progress through the day, and since times of sunrise and sunset change according to the seasons and the country in which one lives, these days Muslims usually have timetables for each region showing the exact moments when the prayer times begin and end.

Since many Muslims go to the mosque to pray together, they also have timetables for congregational prayer, for obvious practical reasons. Many mosques set up clock faces showing these times, five for the daily prayers and one for the special Friday prayer.

Muslims regard it as preferable that men meet together in congregation to pray, but women are generally encouraged to pray in the home. However, there should be nothing to prevent women coming to congregation if they so wish, and it is not compulsory for men to attend every single prayer in the mosque if they prefer to pray elsewhere.

Only one congregational prayer in the mosque is regarded as compulsory, the midday prayer on Fridays – salat al-jama'ah – also known as salat al-jumah. The word 'jama'ah' means 'congregation' or 'gathering', and the word 'jumah' simply means Friday. All adult male Muslims are expected to attend, and are thought to have left Islam if they do not attend for more than three weeks. In Islamic countries all shops and businesses close during this time, so that men can go.

Individual devotion, not priests

There are no priests in Islam. No monopoly of spiritual knowledge or special holiness intervenes between believer and God. No sacrifice or ceremonial is needed to bring the anxious heart nearer to the Comforter. Each Muslim is his or her own priest, no individual being denied the possibility of drawing near to God through his or her own faith. Islam recognizes the dignity and responsibility of every individual human soul; each person faces God on a one-to-one basis, in worship which is a most heartfelt outpouring of devotion and humility before God.

The imam who stands before the congregation leading the prayer is not in any sense a priest, but simply a person who has volunteered to lead, someone who is respected, has good knowledge of Muslim faith, and who knows enough of the Qur'an to recite during the prayer. Most mosques have a regular imam these days, but this is not a compulsory requirement, and any Muslim may lead the prayer in his absence, or when the prayer is being carried out elsewhere, for example, in the home.

If men and women are praying together, the leader is always a man; it could even be a very young man – there are *hadith* showing how a seven-year-old boy led prayers during the Prophet's ﷺ lifetime.

If women are praying together, one of the women leads from the middle of the row, and is in effect a female imam. A male imam would stand just in front of the worshippers, who form lines behind. If there are only two worshippers, the imam stands on the left with the other worshipper on the right-hand side, just a few inches back.

The purpose of prayer

Muslim prayer is intended to purify the heart and bring about spiritual and moral growth. The aims are to bring people close to Allah; to bring a sense of peace and tranquillity; to encourage equality, unity and brotherhood; to develop gratitude and humility; to demonstrate obedience; to train in cleanliness, purity and punctuality; to develop discipline and will-power; to draw the mind away from personal worries, calm down passions, and master the baser instincts.

Preparation for prayer

Niyyah

The first part of prayer is *niyyah* or intention. By closing the mind to all worldly distractions (whether pleasant or unpleasant), the worshipper begins to make ready for prayer. Although prayer can be said at any time in any place, Muslims prepare for *salah* by making their own bodies physically clean, and by selecting a clean place in which to pray, if possible. If one prays in the desert or by the roadside, one is not able to dictate conditions, but in Muslim countries there are usually little areas marked out and set aside for prayer and kept in a clean condition. In the home, or at the mosque, prayer is usually said on a carpet. It may be an individual prayer mat or, at the mosque, the floor is usually carpeted or covered with rush-matting, with lines marked out on it so that the worshippers may arrange themselves in orderly fashion.

Prayer mats are usually small colourful rugs, decorated with abstract designs or depicting some holy mosque. They frequently show the Ka'bah or the mosque at Madinah where the Prophet ﷺ is buried. The only significant point about the design is that it should not depict living beings. Otherwise, any mat will do.

Clothing

Muslims should wear clean clothes for prayer, as far as possible. They remove their shoes, but it is not necessary to remove socks, stockings or tights. Men must be covered at least from waist to knee, and women must completely cover themselves, leaving only face and hands visible, and should not wear perfume.

It is not compulsory for men to cover their heads, but many wear a special prayer cap, sometimes of white lace.

Wudu

There is a difference between everyday washing away of dirt and becoming purified for prayer. Purification (*taharah*) is a mental as well as a physical cleansing. Before prayer, Muslims perform the ritual wash known as *wudu* (some Muslims pronounce it *wuzu*), cleansing certain parts of the body in running water.

The washing is always done in a quiet, prayerful manner, for it is in itself part of the act of worship. While washing, Muslims pray that they will be purified from the sins they have committed by word or deed, that they will be empowered to do good and refrain from evil, and walk on the right path and not go astray.

If water is not available, the worshipper can perform a dry wash known as *tayammum*, which simply involves touching clean earth and wiping over the face, hands and arms in an imitation wash.

Muslims are not required to make a fresh wudu before every prayer if they have remained 'in wudu' between times. Wudu is broken if a person has sexual intercourse, or if any discharge leaves the body (such as blood, seminal fluid, urine or faeces, or wind), or if the person has lost consciousness through sleep or other cause. Women who are menstruating, or are in the days after childbirth, cannot enter wudu and are excused from salah prayer at these times. A full bath, known as *ghusl*, is necessary after sexual intercourse, when menstruation has finished, and after contact with dead bodies.

Qiblah

The *qiblah* is the direction faced during prayer, the direction of Makkah. Muslims usually know its position in advance, but if they are in a strange place they can ask, work it out from the position of the sun, or use a small compass.

There is a consolidating effect in fixing a central spot around which to gather the religious feelings of Muslims throughout the world. Muslims do not believe that God somehow lives at Makkah, or in the Ka'bah sanctuary, or could be 'confined' to any temple made with human hands, much less that they are worshipping the famous black stone set in one of its corners. In the spiritual sense, the true qiblah means to turn the heart in the direction of God – and He, of course, cannot be located in any physical direction whatsoever.

The barrier

It is bad manners to pass in front of someone at prayer. If they are praying in the open, Muslims usually mark off the area of their prayer with a barrier, or *sutrah*, which separates them from any people or animals passing in front of them. The Prophet ﷺ used to stick his staff into the ground, just to the right of him, in case there might be any thought that he was in some way bowing down to it as one might bow down to an idol.

The practice of prayer

The series of movements and accompanying words is known as a *rakah* (pl. *rakat*). These always follow a set pattern.

During the rakah there are eight separate acts of devotion. The first, after *niyyah* (conscious intention), is *takbir* or glorification, the deliberate shutting out of the world and its distractions, delights and miseries. Muslims stand to attention, and raise their hands to the level of their shoulders, and acknowledge the majesty of God. They say 'Allahu Akbar' – 'God is the Most High'.

Second, they place their right hand over the left on the chest, and say in Arabic 'Glory and praise be to You, O God; blessed is Your name and exalted is Your majesty. There is no God other than You. I come, seeking shelter from Satan, the rejected one.'

After this comes the recital of the first *surah* in the Qur'an, *Surah al-Fatihah* – the translation is:

In the name of Allah, the Compassionate, the Merciful. All praise be to Allah (the Almighty), the Lord of the Universes, the Most Merciful, the Most Kind, Master of the Day of Judgement. You alone do we worship, and from You alone do we seek help. Show us the next step along the straight path of those earning Your favour. Keep us from the path of those earning Your anger, those who are going astray.

Next, another passage from the Qur'an is recited, the choice of the prayer leader. It can be long or short, but the Prophet recommended keeping recitals short for public prayers (where people in the congregation might be suffering discomfort, illness, coping with children, or have business to attend to), and whatever length you liked for private prayers.

Next comes *ruku*, the bowing. Men rest their hands on their knees and bow right over with a straight back; women do not bow quite so deeply. This bow is to show that they respect as well as love God. They repeat three times:

Glory be to my Great Lord, and praise be to Him.

The next state is *qiyam*, when they stand up again and acknowledge their awareness of the presence of God with the words:

God always hears those who praise Him. O God, all praise be to You, O God greater than all else.

Next comes the humblest of all positions, the *sujud* or *sajda*. Muslims prostrate themselves upon the ground, touching the ground with their hands, forehead, nose, knees and toes. Their fingers face *qiblah*, and their elbows are raised and not lying on the ground. They repeat three times:

Glory be to my Lord, the Most High. God is greater than all else.

Then they kneel up again in a sitting position known as *julus*, palms resting on the knees in a moment of silent prayer, before repeating *sujud* again.

There is a set number of rakat for each prayer; *fajr*, the dawn prayer requires two, the *zuhr* and *asr* have four; *maghrib* has three and *isha* has four. At the end of the compulsory sequence they pray for all the brotherhood of the faithful, the congregation gathered there, and for the forgiveness of sins. When they pray for forgiveness, they place their right fist on right knee and extend the forefinger. The last action is to turn the head to right and left with the words:

> *Asalaam aleikum wa rahmatullah – Peace be with you, and the mercy of Allah.*

This is known as the *salaam*, and acknowledges not only the other worshippers, but also the attendant guardian angels. Some Muslims can be seen sighing, and wiping their hands over their faces to end their prayer session.

Zakah – the religious tax

> *By no means will you attain to righteousness until you spend (in the way of Allah) out of that which you cherish most.*
>
> (Surah 3:91)

The third pillar of Islam is *zakah* from the word *tazkiyah* meaning 'to cleanse, bless, purify, increase and improve'. Virtually every time Allah asked for the practice of regular prayer to be said by believers, He also asked for Muslims to give material help to those less fortunate than themselves. The Qur'an actually specifies the categories of those people who should be helped by this giving:

> *Zakat are for the poor and the needy, and (to pay) those employed to administer the funds; for those whose hearts have been (recently) reconciled (to Truth); for those in bondage, and in debt; in the cause of God; and for the wayfarer; (Thus is it) ordained by God, full of knowledge and wisdom.*
>
> (Surah 9:60)

Purifying your attitude towards money means being prepared to sacrifice it for God rather than clinging to it selfishly. Zakah discourages hoarding and miserliness. It blesses the wealth from which it is taken, and the person who makes the sacrifice.

Muslims have a duty to look after themselves and their families and dependants; but after that is taken care of, Allah requires that they should look at their surplus money, capital or goods, and give up one fortieth of it (or 2.5 per cent) to God's service, asking neither recompense nor thanks (Surah 26:109). This is a reasonable amount and is not usually a massive sacrifice. However, if the person is extremely wealthy, they can afford to give more.

Basically, Islam is against the idea of hoarding. All of Earth's commodities, including cash, should be in use, or in flow. Any time an individual hoards something, this is disapproved of in Islam, because it is a selfish misuse of that commodity, and deprives others who might be able to put it to use. Zakah taxes collected by an Islamic treasury are used to provide for the needy, including the poor, elderly, orphans, widows and disabled. An Islamic government is also expected to store food supplies in case of famine or other disaster. In effect, it provides for a 'welfare state'.

Sawm – fasting

O believers, you must fast so that you may learn self-restraint.
Fasting is prescribed for you during a fixed number of days,
so that you may safeguard yourselves against moral and
spiritual ills.

(Surah 2:183–4)

The fourth pillar of Islam is to fast during the ninth month of the Muslim year, *Ramadan*. Many Muslims fast at other times too, and some fast one day every week.

The reason Ramadan became so special and significant for Muslims was that it was during this month that Allah chose to call Muhammad ﷺ to be a prophet, and sent down the first revelations of the Qur'an. Therefore, Ramadan is seen as the most significant of months.

Ramadan has basically three aspects – it is a time of physical discipline and self-control, a time for withdrawing from the world and drawing closer to God in peace and prayer, and thirdly, it is a time for making extra effort to reach out to the world, and if possible to touch the lives of others in spreading love, peace and reconciliation.

The physical discipline of Muslim fasting involves giving up all food, liquid, smoking and sexual intercourse during the time from the first light of dawn to sunset, for the entire month. However, it is not just a question of going without food and drink; that is only one aspect of it, and indeed, it is not the most important aspect. Breaking the moral codes of Islam break the fast just as much as eating or drinking.

Long fasts can be very strenuous. In the UK, for example, the fast on 1 July starts at 2.55 a.m. and finishes at 9.40 p.m. demanding considerable self-control. The object of the fast is not to make people suffer, but it is intended to make them realize what it is like to go without, and to share just for a little while the deprivations of the poor, so that a more sympathetic attitude is engendered.

The second aspect is the withdrawal from the everyday world, with all its commitments and anxieties, to deliberately cultivate a peaceful and prayerful attitude of mind.

Muslims spend more time in prayer and study of the Qur'an in Ramadan, many reading through the entire Qur'an. There are special extra voluntary prayers at the mosque each evening when the day's fast ends. These special prayers take about two hours, and are known as *tarawih* (pauses or sections); the Qur'an is divided into 30 sections – so that by the end of the month the entire text will have been recited.

Some Muslims withdraw altogether from ordinary life and go into retreat for the last ten days of Ramadan to devote their entire time to prayer and reading the Qur'an. Men sometimes live and sleep in the mosque in order to do this, and women withdraw from normal life at home.

Laylat ul-Qadr

No Muslim knows for certain which is the night of the Descent of the Qur'an, but traditionally it is celebrated on the 27th Ramadan.

Scholars admit, however, that it could have been any one of the odd-numbered nights during the last ten days of the month, i.e. between the 19th and 29th Ramadan.

A large number of Muslims spend this entire night in the mosque, reading the Qur'an and praying together. Indeed, the mosque is usually completely packed. Muslims believe that if they spend the whole of this night in prayer and meditation, they will be granted the blessings as if they had prayed for a thousand nights.

People excused from fasting

Any person who would undergo real suffering if made to fast is excused from doing it. This applies to people who need to be nourished, such as small children and old people, and expectant and nursing mothers, and those with a medical condition requiring food, liquid or medicine. They perform their fasts by *fidyah*, feeding a poor person twice a day for the month, or paying the cash equivalent.

Hajj – pilgrimage to Makkah

It is the duty of all believers towards God to come to the House a pilgrim, if able to make their way there.

(Surah 3:91)

The fifth pillar of Islam is somewhat different from the other four, in that it involves a complete upheaval of the individual's life for the space of a few days. The *Hajj* (which means 'to set out with a definite purpose') is the pilgrimage to Makkah, the 'Mother-town' of Islam, and it is compulsory for every adult Muslim who can afford it, and who is able to go, once in a lifetime. If any Muslim cannot afford to go, or if it would cause hardship to their dependants, they are excused from making the journey. Some Muslims make the Hajj many times, but this is not encouraged nowadays because the vast number of pilgrims is causing considerable difficulties.

Anyone who wishes to make their pilgrimage more than once is encouraged to go at some time other than the Hajj time, when the pilgrimage is known as the Lesser Pilgrimage, or *umrah*. The true Hajj takes place at a specific time in the Muslim calendar, in the month of *Dhu'l Hijjah*, two months and ten days after Ramadan.

As always in Islam, the real worship and sacrifice is of a spiritual nature rather than the physical show. If, for example, a person who had saved up for Hajj decided to donate that money instead to some unfortunate person in dire need, God would accept the *niyyah* or intention of their Hajj, and it would be counted for them as if they had done it.

Pilgrims have to be Muslim (it is not a tourist attraction), of sound mind and of the age of reason. They must be able to understand the religious significance of the experience. Children might be taken along with the family, but it does not count as their own Hajj until they have reached adulthood. Pilgrims have to have enough money to pay for the trip and keep up all their duty payments towards their dependants. If any person gained money to pay for the Hajj by dishonest means, their Hajj would be invalid.

Pilgrims should realize that they have to be reasonably fit to cope with the strenuous conditions. In view of the numbers and circumstances, many people do pass away while on Hajj – through accident, sickness or old age. Those who leave for Hajj do it knowing they may never return.

The sacred place

Makkah is regarded by Muslims as a specially holy place, and no non-Muslim is allowed to enter it. It is *haram*, which means both 'sacred' and 'forbidden'. When travellers come to Makkah by road, they will arrive at places where their passports will be checked, to make sure that they are genuine Muslim pilgrims and not just curious tourists.

Background to the Hajj

The Hajj pilgrimage celebrates three particular events in Muslim history. The first is the reunion and forgiveness of Adam ﷺ and Eve (there is no doctrine of an original sin passed on to descendants to be redeemed from); the second is the Prophet

Ibrahim 🕮 sacrifice of his eldest son Isma'il 🕮, and the third is the life of obedience of the Prophet Muhammad 🕮.

Adam 🕮 and Eve

According to the Qur'an, when Adam 🕮 and Eve – the original human couple created from the division of the original soul – gave in to the temptation of Satan, they were cast out of Paradise and obliged to wander the Earth in grief, hardship and pain. Not only had they lost God, they had also lost each other, and they were in great confusion and terrible unhappiness. But God had not abandoned them – He watched over them, waiting for the moment when they would turn back to Him and exchange their defiance for the desire for forgiveness. The moment they came to their senses and realized what they had done, God forgave them, and they were reunited on the plain of Arafat, where there is a small hill, Mount Arafat, also known as Jabal ar-Rahman, the Mount of Mercy.

Muslims believe that for any pilgrim to be on that Mount of Mercy on the ninth Dhu'l Hijjah brings total forgiveness of all one's past sins, and enables life to begin again. The stand there is called the *Wuquf*. Nearby, Adam and Eve built a simple shrine in gratitude – the area known as the *Ka'bah* sanctuary. This is now the sacred shrine of Islam, the *qiblah* towards which all Muslims turn in prayer five times per day. The word 'Ka'bah' means 'cube', and it gets this name from the fact that it is a simple, cube-shaped building, some 15 metres high, built of stone blocks. According to Muslim belief, since the first shrine of the Ka'bah (also known as al-Bait al-Haram – the Holy House) was built by the first human, it is therefore the first shrine for the worship of God on Earth.

Ibrahim 🕮 and Isma'il 🕮

The famous story of Ibrahim's 🕮 sacrifice of his son is quite different from that presented in the Bible (Genesis 22:1–14, where God tested his obedience by asking him to sacrifice his son Isaac 🕮).

The Qur'an reveals that Ibrahim 🕮 dreamed that God wanted him to sacrifice Isma'il 🕮 (Surah 37.102). He informed Isma'il 🕮, and the youth agreed that he should do whatever he believed to be God's will.

Tradition added details that heightened the drama. Ibrahim ﷺ, his wife Hajarah and Isma'il ﷺ were all troubled by a stranger – an old man (who was Satan in disguise), who tried to persuade them that they were being misled. Only the devil would ask Ibrahim ﷺ to do such a wicked thing. They all resisted this thought, still believing it was God's will. In the end, all three of them took up stones and threw them at the unwelcome stranger, driving him away.

Isma'il ﷺ was so determined to submit to the will of God that he made his father place him face down, so that he should not be overcome with grief when he saw his face. However, Ibrahim ﷺ had been mistaken and the sacrifice of his son was not God's will. At the last moment God told Ibrahim ﷺ he had long since fulfilled the purpose of that dream, i.e. to show his obedience (37:105).

A ram was sacrificed instead, and became the origin of the 'tremendous sacrifice' of *Eid ul-Adha* at the end of Hajj.

The reward of Ibrahim was that his barren wife Sarah at last gave birth to a son of her own – Isaac ﷺ (Surah 37:100–13).

Later, Sarah's jealousy on behalf of her son caused the family to split up and Ibrahim ﷺ left Hajarah and Isma'il ﷺ to God's care beside the ancient shrine. Here Hajarah was tested again, for although the place was on a caravan route, no water-carrying caravans came by, and they began to suffer severe thirst. When Isma'il ﷺ was on the point of death the angel Jibril (Gabriel) appeared and opened a spring – the well now called Zamzam.

Later the family was reunited and on finding the sanctuary now known as the Ka'bah suffering from flash-flood damage, Ibrahim ﷺ and Isma'il ﷺ rebuilt it together. For the last 4,000 years or so the Ka'bah has always been reconstructed on the same foundations, and the faithful have always gone there on pilgrimage.

The rites of Hajj

It is compulsory for each pilgrim to do four things on Hajj: to enter the state of *ihram* and put on ihram clothing, to perform the circling of the Ka'bah (*tawaf*), to make the stand at Arafat (*wuquf*), and to circle the Ka'bah again, after returning from Arafat. When the pilgrim has done all these four things, he may take the title *hajji* (a female pilgrim is a *hajjah*).

Ihram

Ihram literally means 'consecration', to be *haram* (forbidden to or separated from the world) and it is a special state of holiness, expressed by three things: the complete purification of the body with full bath; the casting aside of normal garments in order to wear special clothes; and the keeping of the ihram rules of conduct.

Women may wear any plain, loose, full-length clothing and a head veil, so that every part of them is covered except the face, hands and feet. They often choose to wear white. Men have to put on two simple pieces of unsewn white cloth, one wrapped around their waist which reaches to their ankles, and one thrown over the left shoulder. They wear nothing else. The object of ihram garments is both purity and equality, single-mindedness and self-sacrifice. Clothing frequently indicates rank, special career or high office; in ihram, no matter how wealthy the pilgrim or how highly born, everyone is dressed the same in these simple unsewn clothes, and they stand before God as equals.

The places where it becomes obligatory to put on these garments are known as *miqat*, around 4 km from the Ka'bah shrine. These days many pilgrims put on ihram even before they board their planes.

Talbiyah

On arrival at Makkah, Muslims start reciting the *talbiyah* prayer, a deeply moving experience as each individual among the thousands and thousands of pilgrims cries to Allah that he or she has arrived, in His service. The translation is:

At Your command, here I am, O God, here I am! At Your command I am here, O Thou without equal, here I am! Thine is the kingdom and the praise and the glory, O Thou without equal, God Alone!

This is the pilgrim's personal answer to the divine call to come.

Tawaf

The first thing all pilgrims are required to do on arriving at the Ka'bah is to encircle it seven times in an anticlockwise direction – the *tawaf*. They do this, no matter what time of day or night they arrive. If they can reach the black stone (*al-hujr al-aswad*), they will touch or kiss it, or raise their hands in salute if they cannot get near. At the end of the circling, they go to the Station of Ibrahim ﷺ to pray two rakat.

Al hujr al-aswad

This is the black stone set in one corner of the Ka'bah. It was said to have been sent down from heaven, and is probably a meteorite. There are numerous traditions about it, one being that it was originally white in colour but it turned black in sorrow at the world's sin (in reality, shiny as it entered the Earth's atmosphere, and black now). It now has a silver surround, but it is still open to the touch. The deep hollow in the middle has been worn away by the millions of pilgrims who have touched and kissed it. It is not, however, an object to be worshipped.

Sa'i

The *Sa'i* is the ritual of running or walking briskly seven times between the two small hills of Safa and Marwah (now a passageway enclosed within the Ka'bah shrine). Any invalids, old people, or those who cannot walk have a special protected wheelchair path down the middle. This ritual is in commemoration of the desperate trail of Isma'il's ﷺ mother, Hajarah, between these two viewpoints, when looking for caravans carrying water. It symbolizes the soul's desperate search for that which gives true life.

The well of Zamzam represents the truth that when all seems lost, God is still present, with healing and life for the soul. The well is still there in a chamber under the courtyard. Pilgrims drink some of the water, and might even collect some in bottles (these can also be bought as souvenirs). Some pilgrims dip their ihram cloths in the water intending to keep them and use them as their shrouds, when they die.

The black cloth over the Ka'bah.

When Muslims have done both tawaf and Sa'i, they have completed *umrah*, the lesser pilgrimage. After this, male pilgrims either shave their heads, or at least cut their hair, and women cut off an inch or so of their hair. Then, they are allowed to put on their normal clothes again.

Mina

On the eighth day of Dhu'l Hijjah, the pilgrims take a full bath and put on ihram again, and proceed to the valley of Mina some 10 km away. This used to be a walk into the desert, but now the town of Makkah reaches virtually as far as Mina, and there are special walkways to make it easier for the huge crowds. It was in the underground walkway that there was a horrific accident with hundreds being suffocated and crushed a few years ago.

There are a few hotels in Mina, but most pilgrims stay in a huge city of tents. Some pilgrims now miss out Mina and take modern transport straight to Arafat, because of the sheer numbers involved.

Wuquf

On the ninth day, all the pilgrims have to reach the plain of Arafat (24 km east of Makkah) and make their stand before God on or surrounding the Mount of Mercy. They have to be there between noon and dusk. Some arrive in good time, but others come rushing up from Mina, having made their dawn prayer there. If they do not arrive for the Standing in time, their Hajj is invalid.

This is really the most important part of the pilgrimage. The pilgrims must stand in the sweltering heat, bare-headed (for men), thinking about God and praying for His mercy. It is a time of great mystical and emotional power, and there is a tremendous sense of release – being totally wrapped in love, totally 'washed', totally cleansed.

It is an amazing sight to see over 2 million pilgrims perform the zuhr and asr prayers here, especially the moments of prostration and total silence as they bow before Allah.

Muzdalifah

By sunset, the pilgrims begin to head back to Muzdalifah, between Arafat and Mina. There they say the maghrib and isha prayers, and collect small pebbles. They arrive back at Mina by the morning of the tenth Dhu'l Hijjah.

Stoning the jamrat

Next comes the ritual of casting their pebbles at Satan, in remembrance of the temptations of Ibrahim ﷺ and his family. There are three pillars set up at representative places, known as *jamrat*, and pebbles are hurled at each one. While doing this, pilgrims rededicate themselves to Allah and promise to do their utmost to drive any evil out of themselves. Muslims are reminded, incidentally, to be careful when hurling these pebbles, so that no one gets hurt.

These days police are in attendance to keep an eye on over-enthusiastic pilgrims. Despite the recent improvements and precautions over 350 pilgrims were crushed to death there in the Hajj of 2006. Some scholars feel it would be better to make this ritual symbolic only.

The sacrifice

After all this, on the tenth Dhu'l Hijjah, the pilgrims who can afford it buy a sheep, goat or young camel, to make their animal sacrifice. This is a three-day festival to commemorate Ibrahim's ﷺ willingness to offer his son's life, but Allah making the substitution of a ram at the last moment.

The animals provide a huge amount of meat to be consumed, so not every person does this. Some pay a cash equivalent. The sacrificer may use two-thirds of the meat for himself and those with him, and a third of it is given away to those too poor to buy their own animal. After the sacrifice the meat is roasted and eaten. The vast number of animals slaughtered presented quite a problem until the Saudi authorities stepped in to organize the disposal of the carcasses. It is impossible for all the meat to be eaten, even if it is shared, so modern technology freezes and processes all the excess meat for distribution further afield.

This is the festival known as *Eid ul-Adha*, the major festival (see Festivals and special days section below), and at the same time as the slaughter, Muslims all over the world are keeping the feast.

Final rites

After this festival, male pilgrims can again shave their heads or shorten their hair, and females trim their hair again. This is done by someone not in ihram. When they return to Makkah they make the final tawaf, and then the pilgrimage is complete.

Festivals and special days

The Muslim word for a festival is *id* or *eid*, from the Arab word meaning 'returning at regular intervals'. The fact that they do occur in a regular cycle is important, for it gives a repeated opportunity for renewal, to forgive enemies, put right quarrels, do things you ought to have done but have perhaps put off or forgotten, and contact people you have not seen for a long time.

Although there are several special times in the Islamic calendar, there are really only two religious festivals. These are *Eid ul-Fitr*, the feast that breaks the fast at the end of the Ramadan month, and *Eid ul-Adha*, the feast of sacrifice that takes place during the Hajj. Eid ul-Adha is the major festival, and Eid ul-Fitr the minor festival.

Both of these feasts are times of celebration and joy, at the express command of Allah as revealed in the Qur'an, when family and friends get together and the local community feels a strong sense of fellowship with the whole Muslim world.

Months in the Islamic calendar are calculated according to a lunar year, therefore each month has 29 days, 12 hours and 44 minutes; the Islamic year is shorter than the solar year by 11 days. The odd 44 minutes of the lunar month means that some years will have 355 days instead of 354. (In a stretch of 30 years, there would be 11 of these 'leap' years.) Therefore, the Islamic festival days are not seasonal, like Christian festivals, and cannot have fixed dates. Each festival comes 11 days earlier each year.

Eid ul-Fitr

Although Eid ul-Fitr is known as the minor festival, many young Muslims enjoy it more than the 'major' one, coming as it does at the end of the month-long fast of Ramadan. It is also known as *Sheker Bairam* (Turkish for 'sweet festival'), *Eid Ramadan* and *Eid ul-Sagheer* (the 'little festival'). It is little because it lasts for three days, whereas Eid ul-Adha lasts for four.

Preparations for the feast begin well in advance, as the amount of food required to feed many guests turning up for meals requires much shopping and advance cooking, usually in gargantuan quantities. Sometimes Muslim shops are so busy that they stay open all night for a few days beforehand.

Many families make decorations and hang them up, or use the trimmings Christians use at Christmas (including tinsel decorations, trees, lights and Santas, but not the cribs commemorating the birth of Jesus). These can now be purchased at any time, all over the Muslim world. The Muslim use has nothing to do with Christmas at all – they are just glittering signs of joy. Sometimes families take the opportunity to spruce up the entire house with a fresh coat of paint, or new curtains or cushion covers.

Gifts or sweets are prepared, and cards made or bought and sent out to relatives and friends. These cards usually show famous mosques, or flowers, or designs, and carry the message Eid Mubarak ('Happy, or blessed, Feast-time').

Special contributions are collected for the poor, the *zakat ul-fitr*. This is not the same as the annual *zakah*, but is charity bestowed as an act of purification for the giver. Zakat ul-fitr is the equivalent of a good meal from each adult member of the family, and should be paid well before the Eid day to ensure that the poor are able to take part in the celebrations, and perhaps to buy some new clothes.

Breaking the fast

The Eid depends on the sighting of the new moon, and this has caused some confusion in countries where the night sky is not always clear. If the new moon is sighted during the evening of the 29th day of the month, that night becomes the first of the new month, but if the moon is not sighted some Muslims fast an extra day to be on the safe side.

Traditionally, the fast is broken by the call to prayer from the mosque, or by the firing of cannons and guns, or the beating of a drum. In Indonesia, for example, the drummers are known as *al musaharati* and they also wake the faithful before every dawn during Ramadan. The time is also announced on radio and TV in Islamic societies, and mosques get the news by radio, telex and telephone.

As soon as the signal comes, there is a release of emotion and much hugging and greeting, handshaking and kissing. The fast is traditionally broken with something very simple, as was the practice of the Prophet ﷺ – usually dates or other fruit, and fruit drinks or milk. After this simple food and drink, the family leaves the table to make the maghrib prayer. The big meal comes later.

In Muslim societies people are so excited and full of the urge to congratulate each other on completing a successful fast that they go out into the streets in party mood to wish each other

'Eid Mubarak'. Visitors go round to call on friends and family, trying to make sure that no one is forgotten.

The Eid day

In Muslim countries there is no work or school on Eid days – everybody has a three-day holiday. In the United Kingdom, Muslim children are granted a day off school, and sympathy from employers towards their Muslim employees is increasing. Others have to content themselves with making the early *salat ul-fitr* prayer, an hour after sunrise, and then getting on with their jobs as usual, looking forward to a good feast in the evening. Salat ul-fitr consists of two rakat with extra *takbirs* (saying of 'Allahu Akbar') and a sermon, usually about giving in charity. There is no call to prayer. Other Eid prayers take place in congregation between sunrise and noon.

Each person going to Eid prayer must first take a full bath or shower, and then dress in new or best clothes. They take a quick breakfast, and hurry to the Eid congregation, which might be at the local mosque, or could be a huge gathering in the largest mosque in the area, or the principal mosque of the city, known as the *Jami'a Mosque*. Sometimes the congregation can be so large it overflows on to the street outside.

After the prayer, everyone greets each other with 'Eid Mubarak' and hugs and kisses, and then the round of visits to friends and family begins. Children get lots of presents and pocket money.

At midday there is a large dinner – the first meal eaten during the day for over a month! It may have to be in several sittings if large numbers of guests arrive. Needless to say, the female members of the family will have put a great deal of effort into preparation of these huge meals. Luckily, the Middle Eastern style of cookery lends itself to these large feasts, and it is fairly easy to expand the food to fit the numbers that turn up.

During the afternoon, families often visit the cemetery to remember all their loved ones who have passed away. They pray for them, and sit by their graves for a while.

The day ends with more visiting and entertaining, going on late into the night.

Eid ul-Adha

This is the major festival, lasting four days, and is celebrated at the end of the Hajj. It commemorates the obedience of the Prophet Ibrahim ﷺ when he was called upon to sacrifice his son Isma'il ﷺ, and his triumph over the temptations of the devil.

Every Muslim takes part in this feast, not only the ones on Hajj. Everyone thinks about the pilgrims who have gone on Hajj, and joins with them in spirit, particularly any who have gone from their own family or community. In Muslim countries, the Hajj is reported on TV for everyone to see.

Eid ul-Adha is a serious occasion, symbolizing the submission of each individual Muslim, and the renewal of total commitment to Allah. The mind is concentrated on the idea of sacrifice and self-sacrifice, symbolized by the actual sacrificing of a sheep, goat, cow or camel.

The animal sacrifice

In Muslim countries this does not usually present a problem as many Muslim men will have been trained in how to slaughter an animal according to the principles of Islam. People in the West are often horrified at the thought of animal slaughter, and regard it as cruelty and a barbaric practice. They are confusing Islamic slaughter with the ancient worshippers of idols who used to consider that their gods needed the ritual sacrifice of blood to give them strength, and so on. This has nothing to do with Islam.

The creature is not slain in any way as a propitiatory sacrifice to God, but as meat for a communal feast. Any person who eats meat should be aware that the meat was once a living animal that was slaughtered specifically so that they could eat. In fact, the Islamic principles of slaughter are to slay the creature in the kindest possible way, with the least amount of pain, and without putting the animal to fear or distress. There is sometimes controversy among non-Muslims over whether or not *halal* (or 'permitted') killing is cruel or kind; Muslims maintain that it is the kindest possible method, ordained by God Himself, and that is why they do it. They do not regard killing an animal by electrocution, or by firing a bolt into its brain (normal United Kingdom slaughterhouse practices) to be kind methods at all.

Muslim slaying should be done with a very sharp knife across the jugular vein, so that the animal loses consciousness immediately. Prayers are said throughout the proceedings. Killing the animal in this way causes the least pain or distress, and the blood drains away easily.

In the United Kingdom, people must have a special licence to slaughter animals, and it is not permitted for Muslims to slaughter their own on their own premises. Licence-holders have to go to the slaughterhouse to sacrifice there on behalf of the community.

Places of worship

Muslims may pray anywhere – in their homes, beside the road or even, in Islamic countries, in busy public spaces such as railway stations. The special place of worship, though, is the mosque, or *masjid*.

Masjid means literally a 'place of sujud or prostration'. In other words, it is any place where someone bows down before God. Muslims kneel and place their foreheads on the ground in the humblest parts of their prostration. This place of prayer does not have to be a special building – any clean place will do. Indeed, the Prophet said:

The whole world has been made a place of prayer, pure and clean.

(Muslim)

Wherever the hour of prayer overtakes you, you shall perform it. That place is a mosque.

(Bukhari)

In Muslim countries it is quite normal to see people praying by the roadside when it is time for prayer. It is also normal for little areas to be set aside for prayer at places like railway stations, often just a rectangular area facing the direction of Makkah, marked out by a few stones, perhaps under a tree, sometimes with a wooden board or a mat to kneel on. You might also see an arrow erected somewhere like a weather-vane, showing the direction of Makkah to the stranger. If possible, there will be a water supply near at hand, for the ritual washing, although *tayammum* (dry washing) is acceptable for the traveller.

The two most important mosques in Islam are the Great Mosque in Makkah and the Prophet's ﷺ Mosque in Madinah. The al-Aqsa Mosque in Jerusalem is usually accepted as the third most revered mosque in Islam, but many countries have a chief mosque, or a special place, which is often spoken of as 'the third most holy site in Islam'. This is because Muslims who cannot go on Hajj often go to their country's special mosque at Hajj time.

The functions of a community mosque

The functions of a community mosque are:

* **Communal prayer** – First and foremost, the mosque is the place where Muslims gather to pray together. The sunnah is for women and small children to pray in lines behind the men in the same prayer space, but in many mosques they have a segregated space such as a balcony or a separate room.

* **Relaxation and company** – Sometimes Muslims feel quite lonely in a non-Muslim community, so the mosque gives them a chance to meet and relax with people who speak their native language.

   The imam can use the premises if he wishes to meet people, discuss problems in the community, or help people with problems concerning their families (or, perhaps, immigration queries).

* **Education** – Most mosques have a collection of books for study, sometimes sufficient to qualify being called a library. Muslims often invite visiting speakers and use the mosque for lectures and talks, or to discuss problems of Muslim law.

The mosque also fulfils an important function as the school (or *madrassah*) where people can study the Arabic language, the Qur'an and various Islamic subjects.

All Muslims are expected to learn as much of the Qur'an as they are able, and for many this is a difficult business as Arabic is not their first language. Boys and girls usually start these Islamic studies at the age of five, and continue until they are 15 or so. It is quite possible to go on being a student for the rest of your life. Some madrassahs are famous universities staffed by the top Muslim intellectuals.

* **Social functions** – The mosque can be hired out for all sorts of functions – meetings, parties for weddings and festival days, birthdays, circumcision parties, or welcome home parties, celebrating the passing of an important exam. These are all joyful functions, and usually involve huge meals. Most mosques will have a good kitchen area as part of the complex, and perhaps a special function room. Some even run a café for the public.

* **Hospital and hospitality** – Sometimes people sleep overnight in a mosque, either on the carpeted floor of the prayer hall or in specially provided facilities. The oldest traditions reveal that many mosques also did service as primitive hospitals, feeding centres, and 'rest-room' facilities. Many still do.

* **Farewells to the dead** – Less happy gatherings are those to mourn the dead and pay the last respects to friends and relatives before burial. The mosque may have an ablutions room where it is possible to administer the last washing to the deceased before shrouding them.

The major features of a mosque

Muslims can convert any sort of building into a mosque – in the UK many old churches, houses and warehouses, even a fire station, have been put to this use by the growing communities. Mosques do not always look like mosques. None of the traditional features is compulsory.

The following are the most typical features.

* The dome gives the impression of space and calm when one goes inside; it also helps acoustically. It is a feature that reminds Muslims of their origins in the Middle East.

* The minaret is a tall tower where the *mu'adhin* gives the call to prayer known as the *adhan*. Throughout the Muslim world this stirring cry is given five times per day, but in non-Muslim societies it is frequently not sounded, so as not to upset and disturb those who would not be sympathetic.

* Atop the dome and/or the minaret one can usually see the symbol of Islam, a crescent moon. Sometimes there is also a five-pointed star which reminds Muslims of the five 'pillars' or obligatory duties of their faith; the moon reminds them of God the Creator, and the lunar calendar which governs Islamic festivals and special days.

* A series of clocks usually shows the prayer times each day – prayer times are flexible when praying on your own, but have to keep to a strict timetable for a congregation to come together.

* Washing facilities. It is not necessary to perform *wudu* at the mosque, and many Muslims prefer to do it at home before going. In the mosque, men and women usually have separate facilities for toilet and ablutions, where there is running water.
  The most common arrangement for wudu ablutions is for a row of taps to be set in the wall over a drain, with stools arranged for people to sit on while they wash their feet. People coming to pray often leave the water to dry by itself and do not use towels.

* Inside the mosque the most noticeable feature is the lack of furniture or decoration in the prayer room. There are no chairs or pews for people to sit on. Everyone sits on the floor.

* There are no pictorial decorations or statues, because representation of this sort is forbidden in Islam as it

encourages idolatry. You will never see any representation of God, angels, or the Prophets.

* Many mosques are extremely beautiful, with richly coloured carpets, different marbles for columns and surfaces, intricately patterned and colourful tiles, carved woodwork, stained glass, beautiful chandeliers, gold-painted ceilings, ornamental calligraphy on texts from the Qur'an, and so forth.

* The carpet in the prayer hall is generally marked out with lines or regular patterns, so that when the prayer lines form, people know where to stand and how much space to occupy. Some massive carpets such as the one at Regent's Park Mosque in London have patterns like individual prayer mats. However, when a large congregation comes together for prayer, they move very close together, shoulder to shoulder, and often literally toe to toe, with their toes touching those of the next person.

* The wall facing Makkah is known as the *qiblah* wall, and set in this wall is a specially decorated niche or alcove known as the *mihrab*.

  When Muslims have taken over existing buildings and converted them into mosques, the qiblah may seem to be in a very odd place, not at all the focal point – this is because it always indicates the direction of Makkah.

* The mihrab is not an altar; it simply points the direction of the Ka'bah, and concentrates the Muslim's mind upon Allah.

  The prayer leader stands in front of the mihrab, which is sometimes known as the 'niche of lights', the symbol for the Divine Presence in the heart. Some mihrabs incorporate a shell shape; the shell symbolizes the 'ear of the heart', and the pearl within is the 'Divine Word'.

* On the right side of the mihrab is the *minbar*, the platform from which the imam gives the *khutbah* sermons. The minbar can be very simple, or highly ornate. The simplest ones are usually just a couple of carpeted steps with a

small platform at the top. Ornate minbars can consist of a high flight of stairs, beautifully carved and decorated.

Imams

The imam is the leader of the mosque. As mentioned earlier in this chapter, there are no priests in Islam. However, whenever two or more Muslims come together to pray, the one with the most knowledge, or the eldest, leads the prayer.

The imam also usually has the job of *khatib*, that is, he delivers the *khutbah* or double sermon at the Friday congregation, and probably organizes Islamic studies for the young people. After the first sermon, the imam will sit down for a few moments, and then give the second. Then the Friday prayer of two rakat follows, and after this people pray individually.

Any person respected by the mosque members, who has studied the Qur'an and hadith, has good knowledge of the faith, and is known for his piety and common sense can be elected imam for the community. In the UK, each mosque elects its own imam. Some imams have become famous teachers, and have rallied the faithful in times of persecution or war.

Visiting a mosque

When visiting a mosque, one should be suitably dressed. For men, this involves being clean, smart and tidy. Muslim men would not go into a mosque with a shirt hanging open, or wearing shorts. For women, it is polite to cover the arms and legs, and wear a scarf or veil over their hair. Muslim women's dress is always modest – transparent, over-tight or too short clothing would be out of place, as would too much make-up or any perfume.

Both men and women should bear in mind that they will probably be asked to sit down on the floor, difficult and embarrassing in tight clothing or short skirts.

On entering the mosque, both men and women take off their shoes and place them in the rack or on the shelves provided. It is not necessary to take off socks, stockings or tights, but polite visitors will make sure their socks are clean and without holes.

Quiet, respectful behaviour is expected at all times. It is considered very bad manners to talk loudly, to call out to someone, to smoke, or to interrupt the devotions of people who might be already praying or reading the Qur'an.

social Islam

For pious Muslims, faith and discipline enter every part of their lives – from their intimate lives with their husbands or wives, through their friendships and their lives as part of the wider community as employees or employer, and even their financial affairs. In all these areas the core Islamic values such as honesty, compassion and respectfulness play an important role. Sobriety and modesty are also key values in interpersonal relations – for both men and women – and these are evident in the Islamic rules on sex, alcohol and dress.

The Islamic treatment of women always attracts a lot of attention from Westerners, who sometimes argue that Islam is essentially repressive of women's rights. This is not true, unless Islam is being abused. While the Qur'an requires modesty of women (just as it does of men), it is also deeply respectful of them and recognizes a profound equality between men and women, even while they may serve different social roles.

Islamic human rights and ethics

Many people seem to spend a great deal of their time and effort demanding their rights, and are frequently discontented whatever they received In Islam, rights are not an end in themselves, but the means to fulfil the duties of life. The human being who is worthwhile contributes to life and shares in the service of humanity, alleviating human suffering and working hard to take care of those in his or her charge. The true Muslim is interested in the economic and scientific advancement of humanity, as well as moral and spiritual well-being.

The basic human rights

All human beings are the creations of God, and loved by Him. Therefore there are certain basic rights which should be shared by the whole of humanity, whether people are Muslim or not. All have the right to be fed, clothed, educated, cared for and buried by the society which governs their existence. Every society contains people whose disabilities prevent them from working, or who are too sick or too weak to earn sufficient wages to secure a decent life. There are children who lost parents, wives who have lost husbands, old people who are no longer able to care for themselves. Any society with the least respect for human dignity would not allow such people to be left neglected and uncared for.

Islam makes it obligatory for the wealthy and able-bodied to support the less fortunate. No society should victimize or terrorize its weak members, or deprive people of liberty for no reason. No society should try to 'brainwash' its members, or attempt to force them to believe things against their natural will, ability or awareness.

These human rights have all been granted by God Himself, and not by any ruler or government, and it is the duty of Muslims to protect these rights actively. Failure to do so results in the loss of these rights, and leads to *tughyan* – tyranny and suffering.

None of you is a true believer until you wish for your brother what you wish for yourself.

(Bukhari and Muslim)

In Islam, human rights include the following specific areas:

* The right to life.
* The right to equality.
* The right to freedom.

Freedom of speech and opinion should be weighed against the offence given to others. Muslims would always object to books, media reporting, TV programmes that vilify the prophets – who are no longer here to speak for themselves. They protest vociferously against films that slur the character of Jesus ﷺ, for example.

People have the right to freedom. Nobody should be kept prisoner without trial and sentence, or enslaved (unless it is a voluntary arrangement to pay off debt), or kidnapped or hijacked. Moreover, people should not be kept in enforced marriages, or by employers from whom they wish to break free.

Islamic ethics

God does not look upon your bodies and appearances; He looks upon your hearts and deeds.

(Bayhaqi)

The aim of Islam is to promote certain values specifically, and deliberately try to reduce or stamp out others.

The key values in Islam include:

* Faith
* Justice
* Forgiveness
* Compassion
* Truth
* Tolerance
* Modesty

The key things that are abhorred are:

* Hypocrisy
* Cheating
* Backbiting and suspicion

* Lying
* Pride
* Envy
* Anger
* Divisiveness
* Excess and extremism

These ethical values are shared with all serious followers of many religions – they are universal values. Islamic ethics could be summarized by this one verse from the Qur'an and this one famous hadith:

> *Goodness and Evil cannot be equal. Repay evil with what is better, then he who was your enemy will become your intimate friend.*
>
> (Surah 41:34)

Women in Islam

> *For Muslim men and women, for believing men and women ... for men and women who are patient and constant, who humble themselves, who give in charity, who fast, who guard their chastity, who engage in the praise of Allah – for them Allah has prepared forgiveness and a great reward.*
>
> (Surah 33:35)

This particular verse was the answer from Allah given in direct response to the Prophet's ﷺ wife Umm Salamah, who asked him one day why the Qur'an revelations never specifically mentioned women.

In Arabic, the word *insan* (man) means 'a human being', 'person', or 'male and female' without a particular gender identification, and thus every instruction given to Muslims in the Qur'an refers to both male and female believers alike unless it clearly specifies otherwise. They have been given the same religious duties and will be judged according to exactly the same criteria. If a verse is intended for men only or women only, this is made clear.

Muslim doctrine holds that women are not in any way inferior beings to men, but were created originally from the same single soul.

O humanity! Have reverence for your Lord, the One who created you from a single soul (nafs) and from that soul He created its mate, and through them He spread countless men and women.

(Surah 4:1)

Women's rights

Muslim women are granted equal, but different, rights in Islam as well as equal responsibilities. Allah gave them the burdens of menstruation and childbirth, and therefore certain privileges and allowances are made for them, such as being excused from salah prayers and fasting while menstruating.

A woman in Islamic law is equal to her male counterpart, just as liable for her actions as a male. Her testimony is demanded and valid in court, her opinions are sought and acted upon, just as the Prophet ﷺ consulted his wives. She has the same duty as a man to become educated and a useful member of the community. To seek knowledge is the duty of every Muslim.

The Qur'an clearly shows Allah's intention to liberate women from injustice by giving them rights not previously enjoyed. Some examples include rights of ownership, decision-making in marriage, divorce and so on. Both Muslim men and women are expected by God to **'enjoin the doing of what is right and forbid the doing of what is wrong'** (Surah 9:71) in all spheres of life, and to act as His vice-regents in ensuring justice, freedom and equality for all. Yet Muslim women have varying roles, rights and obligations depending on the particular society in which they live.

Women and education

Muslim women were/are commanded by Allah to seek education from cradle to grave and from any source available. When Muslim women and girls are refused education this is the very opposite of what the Prophet ﷺ taught. He appreciated forthright women who were not frightened to speak out, or discuss and debate matters. He appreciated women who were educated and had knowledge, who were also kind and compassionate, and hard-working and hospitable. Certainly some Muslim women live in societies that do not stretch to education for girls, but happily, many Muslim women are among the most highly qualified professionals in the world.

In some places Muslim females are not allowed to be taught by men, yet all the women of Madinah were taught by the Prophet ﷺ himself; and moreover, even before his demise, men were also being taught by intellectual women – such as Umm Waraqah, Umm Darda, Shifa bint Abdullah, and the Prophet's ﷺ beloved Aishah, despite her youth.

These days many homes cannot afford the luxury of a housewife. Parents may think of their male offspring as future breadwinners, but ignore the fact that all too often men are unemployed and the females are the breadwinners. Girls are persuading their parents that there is a desperate need for Muslim women to acquire a good education using modern methods and technology, and to achieve useful qualifications.

Educated Muslim women are a necessity. It is highly preferable in Islam for women to be treated by female nurses and doctors, dentists and midwives, and taught by female teachers, and counselled by female lawyers – therefore Muslim women need to train. Muslim women's services are needed – as tailors, bakers, librarians, chemists, engineers, nurses, secretaries, teachers, police, those who work with the mentally ill, marriage counsellors, ambulance drivers, doctors, dentists, midwives, lawyers and so on.

The right of access to the mosques

In the Prophet's ﷺ day, women went regularly to the mosque to pray with the men, despite the attempts of some of those men to keep them away. The Prophet's ﷺ wife Aishah reported: 'I used to set out towards the mosque and observe prayer along with Allah's Messenger; and I was in the row of women nearest the row of men.' (Muslim). The Prophet's ﷺ order to menfolk reluctant to encourage their wives to attend the mosque was: 'Do not forbid the mosques to the women of Allah.' (Bukhari 11.12) 'When a woman asks one of you to go to the mosque, grant this to her.' (Nisa'i 2.32)

Some small mosques are men-only prayer clubs – even turning away travelling Muslim women who arrive looking for a place to pray – when they should function as useful community centres with all sorts of facilities, and not only allow womenfolk to pray there, but to utilize their talents in the general running of the place. These places drive up-and-coming Muslim women to despair, and will no doubt find more and more people voting with their feet, leaving them to head to a community of like-minded souls, and joining other more progressive communities.

Seclusion of women

Seclusion of women was originally nothing to do with Islam but an aspect of social class, both for security and snobbery. Wealthy people were able to afford privacy. These days it is largely Muslim societies where the practice still persists, but extreme seclusion for all women was never asked for by Allah or the Prophet ﷺ, and the hadiths are full of descriptions of active, courageous and hospitable women out and about, entertaining, nursing, or on the battlefield.

The urge for Muslims to seclude women arose from a narrow interpretation of the following verses addressed specifically to the Prophet's ﷺ wives:

> *O wives of the Prophet! You are not like ordinary women. If you fear Allah, don't be too casual in your speech, lest someone with an unsteadfast heart should be moved with desire ... live quietly in your houses, and don't make a worldly display as in the times of ignorance; establish regular prayer and give regular charity, and obey Allah and His Apostle.*

(Surah 33:32–3)

If devout Muslim women choose to regard this as binding upon themselves from the desire to emulate the Prophet's ﷺ wives, all well and good, and they have the right to it, but if they are forced into it, this is an abuse of Islam.

There is no text requiring women to be hidden away at all times, although in many cultures Muslim women are very shy of strangers, and many accept seclusion as one form of piety. In today's world, you can see Muslim women in public in every country and culture, content that in their modest dress and behaviour they are fulfilling any requirement of Islam.

Exploitation of women

Women's honour is highly regarded in Islam, and a woman of any age has the right to be treated according to her position; as a protected virgin, a respected wife and partner, an honoured mother or grandmother.

Islam takes note of the physical differences between the sexes; it does not assume that men and women are 'the same'. Thoughtful allowances should be made to protect women and make them comfortable. Men do not have to endure menstruation, pregnancy, childbirth and suckling children. A Muslim woman has the right to be cared for at times of physical pain and discomfort. Men are not usually harassed because of their attractiveness, or forced to accept sex in order to 'get on', or not lose a job.

In many cultures women have been and still are subjected to all sorts of abuses and restrictions from their menfolk. It is not Islam that causes abuse or oppression of women, but chauvinism and the mingling of Islamic teachings with tribal customs and traditions.

Feminists are calling for re-evaluation of attitudes and practices that, although done in the name of Islam, are actually the result of strong cultural influence, some even contrary to the basic messages found in Qur'an and *sunnah*. They seek to revive the equality bestowed on women in the religion's early years by re-reading the Qur'an, putting the verses in context, and disentangling them from tribal practices.

A woman forbidden from driving a car in Riyadh will cheerfully take the wheel when abroad, confident that her country's bizarre law has nothing to do with Islam. A woman forbidden education or the chance to work in Afghanistan might have been a High Court judge in pre-Taliban days.

Forced marriages may still take place in certain Indian, Pakistani and Bangladeshi communities, but would be anathema to Muslim women from other backgrounds. Female genital mutilation is still practised in certain pockets of Africa and Egypt, but is viewed as an inconceivable horror by the vast majority of Muslims.

Islamic clothing

People who have travelled about the world will be very aware that there are all sorts of styles and garments that qualify as Islamic dress. Basically, the principles are modesty and cleanliness. What people actually wear is very much governed by the society in which they live, but Islamic garments are always modest and, if possible, clean.

The Prophet ﷺ said:

Every religion has a characteristic, and the characteristic of Islam is modesty.

(Ibn Majah)

Men's clothing

There are few particular rules for men's wear, except for pilgrims in *ihram*, and when it comes to the time of prayer. At prayer times, even in the most primitive conditions, men must be covered at least from navel to knee. In ihram male clothing consists of two unsewn sheets of white cloth and nothing else. Otherwise, the only rulings are that men should not wear garments made of silk, unless they have a skin disorder that requires it, and should not wear jewellery other than a wedding ring, which should be made of silver and not gold. Women are allowed to wear gold and other jewellery.

Some Muslims adopt particular styles that indicate affiliation to sects within Islam. Men of the Tablighi-Jama'at, for example, go for long beards, prayer caps, and short trousers that clear the ankles. *Sufis* often have distinctive turbans or robes. The Nation of Islam men wear Western-style suits and bow ties.

Hijab

Hijab means veiling, covering or concealing, and indicates modesty both in dress and behaviour, an expression of piety for all Muslim women. Discussion only arises over the extent of the cover. Muslim women are not expected to wish to display their sexual attributes in public. That is something reserved for their husbands, for whom they should make themselves as beautiful and attractive as possible.

Some Western women may regard Muslim women's dress as dull, and restrictive – but this is not how Muslim women see it. They prefer to dress in beautiful clothing which is graceful but modest, and regard revealing and sexually provocative clothing as pandering to the lowest instinct of the male, and encouraging men to look on women as sex objects rather than equal and independent characters. Women going about in public dressed to stir up male lust are regarded as 'offering the goods' and 'asking for trouble'.

Islam does not require women to wear long black robes and black veils, nor to hide their faces, but travellers will have become familiar with Muslim women so covered in certain places. The requirement of Islam is for Muslim women to cover their bodies from the neck to the wrist and foot. They should not wear garments that show the outline of their private parts. This can be done with any long robes, dresses and skirts, long shirts and trousers, and so on. Various cultures have different standards of modesty; in some Muslim societies colours are more muted than others, head veils less decorative, and so on. The majority of Muslim women cover their heads, and the extreme extent is to cover faces, and to also wear socks and gloves.

Face veils have become an issue in some non-Muslim societies, where masks are traditionally seen as threatening, sinister, or a means of hiding the identity of a criminal or terrorist.

Covering the head

The one item of clothing that usually marks out a woman as a Muslim is the head veil, of any material and in any style, that hides her hair from public view. Head veiling really is not mentioned in the Qur'an, but those who are convinced that it is compulsory are basing their view on the *sunnah* of the Prophet's ﷺ wives, and the hadiths recording that the Prophet ﷺ himself said on one occasion that nothing of a female past the age of puberty should be seen except her face and hands. Muslim women usually do cover their heads with some kind of scarf or veil.

The fact that millions of Muslim women dress modestly but do not cover their heads does not alter the fact that it is a sunnah. Those who do wear some sort of head-cover regard this as part of their discipline of piety, and where there is a resurgence of Islamic faith, women are choosing to wear a scarf in increasing numbers.

Covering the face

There is no text in the Qur'an requiring Muslim women to veil their faces. In desert situations, both men and women cover their mouths and noses automatically as a practical measure. Wearing a face veil without the inclement weather conditions was considered a status symbol in pre-Islamic Arabia and other countries, a form of social snobbery that prevented the common masses from looking at the faces of those of high rank, sometimes men as well as women. Slave women were certainly not allowed to veil their faces. This is not the Muslim attitude.

The face veil (*niqab* or *khimar*) apparently was worn by some Muslim women at the time of the Prophet ﷺ, but did not become widespread for several generations – until conservatives became ascendant.

There are dozens of hadiths where it is obvious that Muslim women's faces could be seen. Aishah commented that she used to draw her veil across her face when she did not wish to talk to strangers.

The verse in the Qur'an used to justify face-covering for women is preceded by one in virtually identical words applied to men – but neither verse mentions faces – rather, it is a euphemism for modest behaviour and self-control. It is never assumed that an honourable Muslim man is supposed to wear a face veil.

Instruct believing men to veil their eyes (i.e. lower their gaze) and guard their modesty; that is more chaste for them. Surely Allah is well aware of their actions.

(Surah 24.30)

It is what he does with his eyes that matters – he is supposed to turn away from female temptation, and not leer or flirt, and to control any feelings of arousal. The Prophet ﷺ excused the first such look, but not the second.

Different cultures, different expectations

Veiling for Muslim women today is complex and varies from place to place. In Saudi Arabia and Afghanistan state law obliges women to cover completely, but that is not the case in Egypt, Morocco or most other Middle Eastern countries. In Tunisia and Turkey the veil is prohibited in governmental buildings like courts, universities, schools, town halls, etc. In Turkey, it is a source of controversy, as it is banned in various places, but both secular feminists and pious Muslim women march for the right of freedom to wear it. In many Western minds the 'cover' is an indication of oppression – an assumption that possibly derives from the West's past experience of its own history of repressive religious states and societies. In the twentieth century many Islamic feminists demanded the right to cast aside even their head-coverings, but today Islamic feminists demand the right to not face discrimination if they choose to wear them.

Islamic diet

In Islam, foods are either *halal* or *haram*. That which is halal is allowed, and that which is haram is forbidden. This is not a matter of likes and dislikes, but of discipline and submission to God's will. As in every other walk of life, Allah gave instructions to guide believers, and even the need to eat is under discipline. Allah created all the goodness of the earth and its produce for humanity to utilize, but requested certain restrictions.

O believers! Eat of the good things that We have provided for you, and be grateful to God if it is Him you worship. He has only forbidden you meat of an animal that dies of itself, and blood, and the flesh of pigs, and that on which any other name has been invoked besides that of God.

(Surah 2:172)

Forbidden foods include:

The strangled, the beast beaten down, the beast that died by falling, the beast gored, and that devoured by beasts of prey ... and anything sacrificed to idols.

(Surah 5:4)

How the food-animal died matters. Islamic slaughter involves *tazkiyah* or cleansing, by dedicating the animal in Allah's name, cutting its throat with a sharp blade and draining the blood. Causing the animal needless pain or slaughtering with a blunt blade is strictly forbidden.

The flesh of the pig, or any pork product, is forbidden. This does not mean a Muslim convert simply giving up sausages, bacon, ham and pork pies. It also means checking whether or not a product includes animal fat, for that fat might well have come from a pig.

In the East, the pig is regarded as a very unclean animal, with good reason, for it gobbles up excrement. In some places it is deliberately used for this purpose. Therefore, no Muslim would contemplate eating it, for it is simply regarded as disgusting. To put a piece of pork on a Muslim's plate would have the same effect as putting excrement on their plate; some Muslims would be physically sick.

Halal shops

Muslims in the United Kingdom usually buy all their meat from halal butchers, or special Muslim shops, not regarding the meat in ordinary butchers'shops to be acceptable. In Muslim countries all meat would be slaughtered by the halal method, so there would not be any problem of finding a supplier. As the Jews follow the same rules of slaughter for their kosher meat, Muslims are allowed to eat meat from Jewish shops, if they wish.

Other foods

All fish, fruits and vegetables are halal, and all grains and seeds. However, Muslims should still check packets for ingredients, for many biscuits, cakes, ice creams and soups contain the fat of animals or animal gelatine. Unless it is kosher or of vegetable origin the gelatine found in many desserts, creams, cake fillings, sweets, commercial yoghurts and other foods is usually made from animal hide trimmings, including those of the pig.

Work and wealth

The economic principles of Islam are to build up a just society in which people behave responsibly and honestly, and are enabled to find honourable employment that is not exploitative, corrupt, pornographic or based on cheating and swindling.

Earning for the family is still the responsibility of the Muslim man in most Islamic societies, although there is no ruling in Islam to prevent women from going out to honourable work, so long as they dress and behave modestly.

The importance of work

It is considered very important that a person does work, and does not stay idle or become a burden to others. It is considered very dishonourable to be a parasite on society, unless, of course, one is unable to work through illness or other handicap. Begging is strongly disapproved of, unless there is no other alternative and it is a case of extreme necessity.

Islam makes a difference between lawful and unlawful methods of earning a living.

No body which has been nourished with what is unlawful shall enter Paradise.

(Ahmad, Darmi and Bayhaqi)

Basically, if someone's means of earning a living hurts another, or results in another's loss, it is haram (forbidden). If it is fair and beneficial, then it is halal (allowed). Obviously, any form of making money that involves dishonesty, deceit or fraud, bribery, robbery, hoarding in order to take advantage of hardship, exploitation, artificial creation of shortages, or anything to do with alcohol, gambling or lotteries, sexual degradation or immoral practices, is forbidden to Muslims.

Workers should be protected adequately from danger in the workplace and not exploited or made to work unreasonable hours, or worked to exhaustion in appalling conditions, with no opportunity to take rest or refreshment. Muhammad ﷺ insisted that:

An employer should not ask an employee to do anything beyond his capacity. If that which the master demands is necessary, the master himself should lend a helping hand to the servant.

(Bukhari)

Riba – exploitation and interest on loans

Making interest on loaned money (*riba*) is regarded as a despicable, capitalizing on another person's misfortune or need, and is totally forbidden by the Qur'an. Charging interest makes rich people richer and the poor poorer, since they are forced into more debt and dependency.

This is why Muslim societies establish their own Islamic banks, which have worked out honourable ways of utilizing deposited money without the system of giving or taking interest on money, according to the complicated Shari'ah laws.

Islamic modes of financing are based on the following principles:

* transactions must be free of *riba* (interest, exploitation). Any form of exploitation in trade, e.g. raising prices at times of shortage, counts as *riba*
* *haram* (Islamically illegal) goods and services cannot be produced or consumed
* activities or transactions involving *gharar* (speculation, chance) must be avoided
* *zakat* (the compulsory Islamic tax) must be paid.

Many mainstream banks are now considering how to make themselves 'Muslim-friendly'. In fact, customers are attracted by Islamic banking and in the next decade conventional banks may lose 30–40 per cent of their customers to Islamic banks or those that conform to Islamic regulations. Several top conventional banks have already designed commercial mortgage equivalents for use by Muslims.

Sex

Sex is regarded in Islam as the gift of Allah that gives the human being, in a small way, the experience of the bliss of Paradise, in advance. It is a basic and fundamental urge in human beings, and in the search for sexual fulfilment people can give each other great joy and happiness, but it can also give enormous scope for great despair, hurt, and embarrassment.

Interest in sex starts early, and many youngsters become sexually active as they enter their teens. The youngest age for marriage in the UK is at present 16, but promiscuous unmarried sexual intimacy has now become commonplace, despite the dangers of disease, AIDS and unwanted pregnancies.

Youngsters usually experience a rampant urge for sex when their hormones get going at puberty. Muslim societies have traditionally preferred to see youngsters married at the onset of puberty, rather than risk illicit relationships and unwanted pregnancies. This way they can gratify their desires as much as they like, but within the marriage relationship.

Celibacy and promiscuity

Since sex is a creation and gift of Allah, Muslims cannot regard it as evil and unclean, or that it should be resisted and suppressed. People who choose to be celibate for religious reasons are not approved of in Islam; celibacy is seen as a form of ingratitude towards Allah which might lead to a dangerously stressed, repressed or perverted personality.

However, a celibate person who is quite content, and perhaps channelling their energies into study or research, or concentrating on doing good to others, is in no way sinful.

On the other hand, the gratification of sexual urges without moral considerations is also regarded as an abuse of Allah's intention; Islam seeks for sexual desires to be satisfied, but that the individual and the family are protected from dangerous consequences.

The practice of marriage is seen as the 'fortress' that protects people from being lured into immoral ways by their passionate urges. Sexual promiscuity is usually referred to in Islam as *zinah*, whether it refers to fornication (sex before marriage) or adultery (sex outside marriage after marriage).

Homosexuality

This topic presents a problem for Muslims living in places where homosexuality has become not only acceptable in law, but is increasingly socially acceptable. Persons of the same sex having sexual relations was forbidden by Allah in the Qur'an and in a revelation to the Prophet Moses ﷺ.

> *You satisfy your lust with men (homosexual) instead of women. Indeed you are a nation that has transgressed beyond bounds.*

> (Surah 7:81)

In Islam, if a person is born homosexual, this is not regarded as simply being just another version of 'normal' but as a disadvantage and a test, much the same as being born blind or deaf. God's law requires all sexuality with another person to be within the marriage relationship. This is a very hard test for many people, of both sexes, for all sorts of reasons, homosexuality being only one of them. Those who can control themselves and live within Islamic law are greatly to be commended for the sacrifice and control. 'Sleeping around' is as forbidden to homosexuals as it is to heterosexuals.

Private sexual behaviour is a matter for individual consciences, and no person has the right to hound or victimize another for what is done in private between consenting adults. If a Muslim homosexual chooses to take a same-sex partner, it is a matter between his/her own conscience and the Almighty, and will be judged in the Life to Come. Allah knows best if this sin is worse than taking forbidden substances in private, or choosing to be spiteful or cruel. He is the Judge, and knows all the circumstances.

Muslims cannot accept that homosexual couples have the right to 'engineer', adopt, or raise children, in what are seen as unnatural circumstances.

Sex within marriage

The Prophet ﷺ said:

When a husband and wife share intimacy it is rewarded, and a blessing from Allah; just as it would be punished if they had indulged in illicit sex.

(Muslim)

Having sexual intercourse with one's wife is sadaqah (loving charity).

(Abu Dawud)

Sexual intimacy becomes *sadaqah* if performed for the sake of Allah – which means performed with skill, care and unselfishness, placing the happiness and satisfaction of the spouse before one's own gratification.

Sex is encouraged and blessed between loving spouses so long as what is done does not hurt, abuse, exploit or denigrate one's partner. In an Islamic marriage, neither partner should ever try to force the other one to do anything which is distasteful or unpleasant or painful to them. Marital rape should never take place, or abuse of the wife.

Sexual education

Muslims do not feel that instruction from strangers (whose own personal morals they do not know, or they do know and disapprove of) is a good thing, hence there is much resistance to sexual education programmes in schools. Also, it is not seen as good or necessary to invade young minds with sexual knowledge before they are mature enough for it. An innocent childhood is much preferred.

However, wives and husbands have a duty to make their marriages as happy as possible and, therefore, although Muslim youngsters are protected as much as possible from exposure to the sexual experimentation now common in the West, it is their duty to know how to please their partners, and to strive to do this with the same Islamic dedication that they strive to do their best for Allah in any other sphere of life.

Drugs, alcohol and other substances

Any substance which intoxicates is known in Arabic as *khamr*, and is forbidden to Muslims. The word '*khamara*' means 'veiled, covered or concealed'.

Alcohol

At the time of the Prophet ﷺ, alcohol was consumed in large quantities, and its antisocial effects were very well known. Allah's prohibition, interestingly enough, took human weakness into account, and was given in stages over quite a long period of time. First, it was pointed out that good and evil could come from the same thing; both nourishing and harmful products can actually come from the date palm or the vine. The harm of khamr far outweighed the good, but people were left to make their own decisions (Surah 2:219).

Next came the request that Muslims should not be intoxicated when they come to prayer:

> *O believers! Do not come to prayer with a befogged mind, but come when you can fully understand all that you are saying.*
>
> (Surah 4:43)

Finally came the order, the complete prohibition:

> *O believers! Intoxicants, gambling and trying to foretell the future are the lures of Satan; if you wish to prosper, you must keep away from these things. It is Satan's plan to stir up enmity and hatred in your midst with them.*
>
> (Surah 5.90-91 – see also Surah 5.93)

As news of the revelation spread like wildfire, the Muslims poured away any alcohol they were drinking and got rid of their stores; no 100 per cent Muslim has touched alcohol ever since. Not only that, but Muslims should not sell it, buy it for others, give it as a gift, or work where it is served.

There is no penalty laid down in the Qur'an for drinking alcohol, but the mildest punishment laid down for slander and abuse was a flogging, and since alcohol often makes people abusive and slanderous, flogging is sometimes ordered for publicly offensive drunken behaviour in some countries. It is not part of Shari'ah law to pry into private dwellings or spy on people, but any antisocial, threatening or dangerous behaviour caused by alcohol that is witnessed is always dealt with.

Drugs

The plant world is full of substances which affect the human body and mind, and nowadays the medical profession manufactures artificial substances also, to give similar effects. Their use to provide cures for illness is not forbidden in Islam. However, many drugs, such as marijuana, cocaine, opium and nicotine – powerful intoxicants which affect the human mind – are all classed as khamr. They are frequently misused in a harmful way, totally in opposition to the spirit of Islam.

Drugs are used to escape from the pains and distresses of life, or to indulge in exciting fantasy experience and artificially induced euphoria. Those who experiment often find themselves on the downward spiral to crime, physical decline, insensitivity and depravity. The Muslim general principle against drugs misuse is the same as for alcohol – Allah owns our bodies, and anything which harms or injures them is haram.

Smoking

Millions of Muslims smoke. However, it is obvious that if one extends the principle of not doing harm to oneself or others, then smoking can never be an approved exercise. Non-smokers have the right to breathe clean air, unpolluted by others. Muslims, if they must smoke, should do so with discretion and not damage other people's lungs, furnishings, or set a bad example to the young, or encourage those who have given up to start again. By analogy with the rules for other harmful substances, it is really haram even if not declared so.

Problems for Muslims living in the West

Muslims of every age and ethnic origin may find living in the West challenging. Western values are based on a forthright individualism and liberalism that are profoundly contradictory to the more community-based values of Islam. The overtly sexualized culture of the West, in particular – expressed everywhere from advertisements to dress and open displays of passion – can be deeply embarrassing or even distressing to Muslims, especially those who have been bought up in a different culture. Younger, second- and third-generation Muslims have to find a way of negotiating these difficult cultural differences.

Westerners very often fail to understand the values of Islam and rely on the negative stereotypes that are often pedalled in the Western media. However, the calamity of the 9/11 attacks and other terrorist incidents have nothing to do with the core values of Islam and the everyday piety of Muslims, and should not be allowed to colour relations between Westerners and Muslims living both at home and abroad.

Islam is the fastest-growing religion in the West at the present time, and the number of Muslims in the UK, for example, has now reached around the 2 million mark.

Balancing the converts and number of Muslims born into already Muslim families are the Muslim-born men and women who find the Islamic life too much for them and, in the freedom of Western society, choose to abandon it. It is too early to guess how many of these will come back to their roots in later life.

Some of the problems

Education

There are lots of issues to do with education.

* Muslims prefer education to be segregated for boys and girls at puberty. Muslims prefer their girls to be taught in an all-female environment, and vice versa, and even when they are sent to single-gender schools, if these are available, there is still the question of the gender of the teacher. Muslims would prefer female teachers for girls, and male teachers for boys. They would also prefer at least some of the teachers on the staff to be Muslim by faith as well.

   For these reasons, many Muslims are now attempting to set up their own schools, and encouraging intelligent girls to take up further education so that there will be a good supply of qualified female Muslim teachers.

* Muslims prefer their girls (including white western Muslim girls) to cover their arms and legs and wear *hijab* if possible. Some schools do not allow this, and some countries (notably France) insist upon state schools being secular, and wearing hijab has become an issue. But generally the situation has eased in the West, and most schools will now allow Muslim girls to wear trousers or long skirts as part of their school uniform.

   Varieties of Islamic clothing have caused confusion; in 2005, for example, when one girl at a school that already allowed *shalwar-qameez* and hijab claimed that her faith required her to wear a *jilbab*, it drew attention to the fact that female Muslims define Islamic clothing differently. A jilbab is an outdoor covering garment, more typical of Somali ladies than Pakistani ones.

* Mixed sports lessons, especially mixed-gender swimming, are not approved of, and Muslim girls are not encouraged to wear revealing swimsuits. For most sports, a track suit is approved, or some modest covering such as a bodysuit with shorts worn over it to 'veil' the private parts.

* If non-Islamic religious education is compulsory in school, this can be another problem area. If the school presents a wholly Christian syllabus, the Muslim child may suffer from the notion that Islam is 'wrong' or that everyone else thinks it is 'wrong', which is depressing. Even where a multi-faith syllabus is taught, there is still the danger of faiths other than Christianity being 'talked down', or taught by people who know hardly anything about them and, in fact, teach them wrongly.

* Non-Muslims do not usually realize that Muslim children are also studying at madrassahs, sometimes every night, over and above their normal school studies and homework.

* Many Muslims now realize that they must establish proper academic Muslim schools in the West, but it is an uphill struggle; there is no tradition of them, and there is active resistance to them from fear they will become breeding grounds for extremism.

Such schools would be expected to deliver the full state curriculum, plus the Islamic studies, in a calm and devout caring atmosphere. New schools have struggled to produce the required standards of staffing, building or curriculum, and some have languished at the bottom of league tables – but there has been a huge surge of commitment, skills and finances, and now many Islamic schools head the league tables. The Leicester Islamic Academy, for example, has achieved a 100 per cent success rate in A* to C passes at GCSE.

Work and worship

Many Muslim males would like to attend the compulsory Friday prayers at the mosque, but are not able to leave school or their workplace. Some employers are more sympathetic than others about the hour or so an employee would be missing from work depending on travelling time. The actual gathering is usually about 30 minutes. At school, it is sometimes possible for Muslim youngsters to gather together to pray, but there are not always facilities for this, or for the washing that comes before prayer.

Many Muslims have to do their best to enjoy their Feast Days without being excused from work or school.

Music

Some Muslims believe that all music is disapproved of or even forbidden in Islam, and some ban all instruments except drums, but will accept songs (*nashid*) for the unaccompanied voice.

Certain types of music are certainly disapproved of as they lead towards the *haram*:

* Pop music with sexual lyrics or sexually provocative rhythms.
* Nationalistic and jingoistic music ('God save the Queen' is acceptable, 'Rule Britannia' is not).
* Music which is intended to stir up tolerance for haram substances or behaviour.

Yet there is no ban mentioned in the Qur'an and it therefore falls into the category of that left to the conscience of the individual.

Medical treatment

Muslims prefer women to be treated by women, and men by men, and this is not always possible in hospital situations. However, it is usually possible to choose one's general practitioner (GP). Hospitals are not always very sympathetic to mass visiting from large families, or relatives bringing in (and eating together) familiar spicy food, and there is sometimes a language problem, with very frightened patients unable to understand what is going on, although nowadays people can usually be found who can speak the Asian language of most local Muslims.

Racism, Islamophobia and intolerance

Since the end of the Cold War and the collapse of Communism, and following some appalling acts of terrorism (e.g. suicide bombings), many Muslims feel they are being demonized as the world's major enemy of peace and stability. Many non-Muslims now seem to mistakenly equate Islam with terrorism because of the behaviour of a small number of extremists and individuals duped for political or criminal ends. Muslims are naturally distressed that the nature of Islam as a religion of reason, tolerance and justice does not reach people as it should.

Muslim fears and conspiracy theories

The distortion of the image of Islam and Muslims takes a variety of forms. Occasionally, it genuinely results from reporters' ignorance of Islam. Very often, however, it does seem to represent a deliberate effort by certain news agencies and reporters who use their free speech to discredit Islam and defame Muslims by deliberately distorting Islamic world views and practices with half-truths and downright lies. They associate the views and practices of fanatical groups and individuals with Islam itself, and give out subtle messages and tactics by the use of such phrases as 'Muslim bomb' or 'Islamic terrorism', whereas violence by Christian individuals and groups is rarely referred to as 'Christian terrorism' or a 'Christian army'.

The vast majority of criticisms of Islam made in the media are not actually criticisms of Islam at all, but of that weird type of Islam promoted by sectarian and bigoted people. It is the responsibility of the Muslim community itself to present Islam accurately, so that the small minority of those who seem to enjoy embarrassing all other Muslims with their narrowness of vision may be seen in perspective.

Let us hope that in the twenty-first century a better knowledge and understanding of Islam will enable all those who believe devoutly in God and a life to come to draw closer together in faith and love, and support each other in their efforts to spread the peace, love and compassion of God on earth.

Notes